## AUTORI

**Paolo Crippa** (23 April 1978) has cultivated his passion for Italian history since high school. His research interests are focused mainly in the field of military history and in particular on italian armored units from the 30s until the end of World War II. In 2006 he published his first volume, "I Reparti Corazzati della Repubblica Sociale Italiana 1943/1945", the first organic research carried out and published in Italy on the subject. In 2007 he published "Duecento Volti della R.S.I." and in 2011 " Un anno con il 27° Reggimento Artiglieria Legnano". He regularly contributes to several journals: Milites, New Historica, SGM - World War II, Batailes & Blindes, Armoured Vehicles and history of the twentieth century, Mezzi Corazzati, both as an author, or in collaboration with other researchers. He published with the editor Mattioli 1885 in 2014 "Italy 43 – 45 – Civil War improvised AFV's" (2014), "Italian AFV's of the Civil War 1943 - 1945" (2015) and "Italy 43 – 45 – AFV's and MV's of co-belligerent units" (2018).

**Carlo Cucut** was born in Nole (TO) in 1955. He cultivated a passion for history as a boy and over the years has deepened this interest by dedicating himself to historical research. He published articles in the italian magazines: "Storia del XX Secolo", "Storie & Battaglie", "Milites" and "Ritterkreuz". He published various volumes for Marvia Edizioni: "Penne Nere on the eastern border. History of the Alpini's Regiment "Tagliamento" 1943-1945 ", winner of the "De Cia" Award; "Attilio Viziano. Memories of a war correspondent "; "Armed Forces of RSI on the eastern front"; "Armed Forces of RSI on the Western Front"; "Armed Forces of RSI on the Gothic Line"; "Alpini in the City of Rijeka 1944-1945". For the Trentino Modeling Group he published "The armed forces of RSI 1943-1945. Land forces ".

## PUBLISHING'S NOTES

None of unpublished images or text of our book may be reproduced in any format without the expressed written permission of Luca Cristini Editore (already Soldiershop.com) when not indicate as marked with license creative commons 3.0 or 4.0. Luca Cristini Editore has made every reasonable effort to locate, contact and acknowledge rights holders and to correctly apply terms and conditions to Content.

Every effort has been made to trace the copyright of all the photographs. If there are unintentional omissions, please contact the publisher in writing at: info@soldiershop.com, who will correct all subsequent editions.

Our trademark: Luca Cristini Editore©, and the names of our series & brand: Soldiershop, Witness to war, Museum book, Bookmoon, Soldiers&Weapons, Battlefield, War in colour, Historical Biographies, Darwin's view, Fabula, Altrastoria, Italia Storica Ebook, Witness To History, Soldiers, Weapons & Uniforms, Storia etc. are herein © by Luca Cristini Editore.

## LICENSES COMMONS

This book may utilize part of material marked with license creative commons 3.0 or 4.0 (CC BY 4.0), (CC BY-ND 4.0), (CC BY-SA 4.0) or (CC0 1.0). We give appropriate attribution credit and indicate if change were made in the acknowledgments field. Our WTW books series utilize only fonts licensed under the SIL Open Font License or other free use license.

For a complete list of Soldiershop titles please contact Luca Cristini Editore on our website: www.soldiershop.com or www.cristinieditore.com. E-mail: info@soldiershop.com

Title: **THE DIVISIONS OF THE ARMY OF THE R.S.I. 1943-1945 VOLUME 2 - 3rd DIVISION "SAN MARCO" , 4th DIVISION "MONTEROSA"** Code.: WTW-025 ENG By Paolo Crippa & Carlo Cucut
ISBN code: 978-88-93277686 First edition July 2021
Text: English Nr. of images :73 dimensione: 177,8x254mm Cover & Art Design: Luca S. Cristini

**WITNESS TO WAR (SOLDIERSHOP)** is a trademark of Luca Cristini Editore, via Orio, 35/4 - 24050 Zanica (BG) ITALY.

WITNESS TO WAR

# THE DIVISIONS OF THE ARMY OF THE R.S.I. 1943 – 1945 - VOLUME 2
## 3RD MARINE DIVISION "SAN MARCO"
## 4TH ALPINE DIVISION "MONTEROSA"

---

PHOTOS & IMAGES FROM WORLD WARTIME ARCHIVES

PAOLO CRIPPA - CARLO CUCUT

BOOKS TO COLLECT

# CONTENTS

**3rd Marine Infantry Division "San Marco"**..................5
   Organization chart
   5th Marine Infantry Regiment..................11
      1st Battalion
      2nd Battalion
      3rd Battalion
   6th Marine Infantry Regiment..................16
      1st Battalion
      2nd Battalion
      3rd Battalion
   3rd Artillery Regiment..................22
      I Donned 75/13 Group
      II Hippotrained 100/17 Group
      III Hippotrained 100/17 Group
      IV Mechanical towing unit 149/19guns
   3rd Arditi Exploring Group..................25
   Divisional Units..................26
      Raccolta Battalion
      "Valli" Tactical Group
      Train Escort Department
      Divisional Depot "San Marco"

**4th "Monterosa" Alpine Division**..................57
   Organization chart
   1° Reggimento Alpini..................62
      Reparti Reggimentali
      Battaglione "Aosta"
      Battaglione "Bassano"
      Battaglione "Intra"
   2° Reggimento Alpini..................65
      Reparti Reggimentali
      Battaglione "Brescia"
      Battaglione "Morbegno"
      Battaglione "Tirano"
   1° Reggimento Artiglieria Alpina..................66
      Batteria Comando Reggimentale
      1° Gruppo Artiglieria "Aosta"
      2° Gruppo Artiglieria "Bergamo"
      3° Gruppo Artiglieria "Vicenza"
      4° Gruppo Artiglieria "Mantova"
   Gruppo Esplorante Divisionale "Cadelo"..................74
   Divisional Units..................75
      Training Battalion
      "Ivrea" Battalion
      Pioneers Battalion
      Connections Battalion
      Transportation Battalion
      Divisional Antitank Company
      Health Department
      "Vestone" Battalion
      "Saluzzo" Battalion

**Bibliography**..................97

# 3RD MARINE INFANTRY DIVISION "SAN MARCO"

On the basis of the Keitel-Canevari agreements of 16 October 1943, the 1st Grenadiers Division was established at the Grafenwohr field. From 24 October the Italian soldiers began to converge at the camp, arrivals that will last until almost the end of November for the officers and non-commissioned officers, until the end of December for the troops. The first nucleus of the future "San Marco" Division consisted of a dozen officers from the "Brenner" Division, a hundred gunners from the same Division, two Blackshirt Battalions from Greece, the Company of the 3rd Grenadier Battalion of return from the funeral honors rendered to King Boris in Sofia in August, as well as by soldiers from other Corps and Services. At the end of October, 400 gunners and 32 officers under the command of Captain Viviani arrived from the Hohenstein internment camp. On November 24, General Princivalle was given the task of assuming the command of the 1st Grenadiers Division, ordering him to reach Grafenwohr and to begin the constitution of the Nuclei from which the Departments would be created. The training program included a preliminary phase and three subsequent phases, the first, in which the Officers and Minors were trained with German instructors, the second, where the recruits from Italy were trained by the Italian instructors trained in the first phase , the third, where, upon the Division's return to Italy, the instructors trained in the second phase would train new departments with the recruits from Italy. At the beginning of January 1944 the 1st Period training began for the approximately 3,500 men present; in Italy, General Princivalle proposed transforming the newly formed Division into a Division that would perpetuate the traditions of the "San Marco" Navy Infantry Regiment, obtaining the sending to the Grafenwohr field of 1,900 men from the Xth Flott-MAS and another 1,200 from the Depot of the Infantry Regiment of Marina "San Marco" of San Donà di Piave. On 9 February on the Marschfeld of Grafenwohr the Official and Minor cadres and the troops of the new 1st Grenadier Division lined up to take the Oath of Loyalty to the Republic, in the presence of the Commanding General and the German Generals of the D.V.K. At the end of February 1944, the Division changed its name to that of the 3rd Italian Grenadiers Division. The training, under the constant, inflexible and repetitive order of the German instructors, continued in compliance with the program defined at the start, while the influx of recruits from the 1924 and 1925 classes and volunteers continued from Italy. On March 21st the departures of the personnel of two Artillery Groups began, on the 25th it was the turn of the Tank Hunters Company and the Transport Battalion, on the 26th the remaining two Artillery Groups. On March 29, the strength of the Division totaled 11,400 men. On March 30, the II Arditi Battalion left, the only organic Department already established as it was the II Arditi Battalion of the dissolved X Regiment, reconstituted under the orders of the ancient Commander and integrated by new volunteers, who was framed in the Division as an Exploring Unit . From 2 to 4 April another 3,000 men left for Grafenwohr, on 9 April the Corvette Captain completed the dispatch of personnel with the departure of the 8th echelon. On April 20, in relation to a decree of the Duce of December 16, 1943 published in Italy on that day, the Division changed its name to the definitive name of the 3rd "San Marco" Marine Infantry Division. It is therefore from that date that the "San Marco" Division officially became a Navy Infantry, despite the fact that over 60% of its staff belonged to the ground lever and the Exploring Group was formed by Arditi. On April 24, the "San Marco" was visited by surprise by the Duce and by Marshal Graziani, this visit had beneficial influences on the morale of the men, subjected for months to exhausting training and eager to return to Italy. The training of the recruits then continued, as foreseen by the 2nd Period, then, on July 18, 1944, the second visit of the Division by the Duce and Marshal Graziani took place, who delivered the War Flag to the 5th and 6th

Infantry Regiment. Navy and the 3rd Artillery Regiment. From the day after, the quarterly officers of lodging began to leave for Italy, with the task of preparing the return of the Division. On July 25th the operations of loading materials on the railway trains began, from the 26th it was the turn of the first echelon, the departing force was 15,325 men. Between the end of July and the beginning of August, while the convoys, units and departments already on site were arriving in the Ligurian Riviera di Ponente, they began the reconnaissance for the deployment and improvement of the quartering offices. On 7 August it was possible to say that the deployment of the "San Marco" Division, inserted in the Liguria Army, whose command was entrusted to Marshal Graziani, was now completed, located in the Riviera di Ponente in order to prevent disembarkation and control the rolling stock and passes that , through the Ligurian Apennines, lead to the Po Valley. The I and III Coastal Position Artillery Group, an armed train and some German batteries located around Savona also operated directly under the Division. The Departments were deployed from Varazze to Villanova d'Albenga facing the sea and in the Ligurian hinterland along the Val Bormida up to the border with Piedmont with the 5th Regiment deployed in the western sector and the 6th in the eastern sector. The 1st Group of the 3rd Artillery Regiment, the III Exploring Group and the 103rd Sanitarian Company, from that date, were sent to the Imperia area under tactical dependencies of the 34th Infanterie-Division, where they were employed in the anti-partisan struggle, especially with the Exploring Group. As soon as the first quartermaster quarters returned to Italy, the ambushes and attacks on individuals or groups of marines immediately began, attacks that led to a daily dripping of losses and wounded. The phenomenon of desertions also began which, in a short time, assumed worrying dimensions with cases of abandonment of positions that affected entire principals. To deal with this phenomenon, the Division Command used the strong way, issuing dozens of death sentences by shooting, however, obtaining poor results. From August 28, officially from September 5, the Division Command was assigned to General Amilcare Farina, who had the difficult task of making the "San Marco" a viable and combative military unit back. General Farina immediately began a continuous series of reconnaissance between the departments and inspections of the individual principals, collecting impressions from the individual marines, verifying the strength of the departments, the quality of the officers, and consequently issuing the agendas and the mandatory provisions that , after a short time, they began to bear fruit. Thanks to the assiduous work, the dynamism, the ability to command, the continuous control over all the activities of the dependent departments, the relationship established with the DVK, the honesty and frankness, sometimes rough but always punctual, General Farina succeeded to take back the "San Marco", making it return to the Division on which many hopes had pinned. Technically very prepared, he raised several times with the German allies the question relating to the deployment of the Division, judged to be too vast and deep, the dislocation of the artillery, the lack of replacements and means, always renouncing reprisals that would not have helped the Division, but only harmed civilians and benefited the partisans. From 20 October the II Battalion / 6th Regiment was transferred to the dependencies of the "Monterosa" Division and transferred to the Garfagnana front, followed, from 27 December, by the III Battalion / 5th Regiment which was transferred, under the 232nd Infanterie-Division , always on the southern front. Following these transfers, the deployment of the Division was restricted, being more directed towards the hinterland along the rolling stock that led to the Sella di Cadibona and Passo dei Giovi, the main folding routes of the San Marco and the Italo-German departments in the area. of Western Liguria. Throughout the operational cycle carried out in Liguria, the "San Marco" never had opportunities to fight against the Allies, apart from the two Battalions sent to the Garfagnana front, but carried out only activities of garrison and control of the territory, rolling stock and railway lines, with roundups and cleaning operations, carried out especially by the daring of the Exploring Group, together with other Italian-German departments or independently. On April 25, 1945, the "San Marco" Division began its withdrawal towards Piedmont and the Po Valley, first reaching Acqui, then continuing on the 27th towards Alessandria. Some Departments continued towards Valenza and Mortara where they crossed the Po and formed a bridgehead. On the 28th, the Command moved to Valenza, while some Departments crossed the Ticino heading towards Vigevano, which was crossed. On 29 April the Command moved to Valmadonna, where it was reunited with the Departments of the 6th Marine Infantry Regiment and with the Departments of the III Artillery Group P.C., to then reach Alessandria in prison of war. The units of the 5th Regiment, together with the 3rd Artillery Regiment, the Division Services Command, the Valli Tactical Group, the III Transport Battalion and most of the Divisional Departments, surrendered on April 30 in Magenta. The Pioneers Battalion also surrendered on 30 April in Magenta, while the Exploring Group is to be considered dissolved on the night of 1 May 1945 in Magenta. The II Battalion / 6th Regiment and the III Battalion / 5th Regiment followed the fate of the Divisions where they were posted. The Divisional Depot of Brescia surrendered on April 28 in Lumezzane to the C.L.N. local. It is superfluous to remember that even for the soldiers of San Marco the surrender agreements, signed with the partisans, were largely disregarded and hundreds were shot, we cite for example the soldiers of the Brescia Depot and those of Monte Manfrei.

## Organization chart[1]

- Commander: Brigadier General Aldo Princivalle, then Brigade General (Division since January 1945) Amilcare Farina
- Officers: Lieutenant Berger, Lieutenant Colombini, Lieutenant Grandi
- Chief of Staff: Lieutenant Colonel s.S.M. Guido Beretta, then Lieutenant Colonel Rinaldo Rossi, finally Major .S.M. Achille Mainella
- Office 1 / A Operations: Lieutenant Colonel s.S.M. Ferrari, then Lieutenant Colonel s.S.M. Beretta, finally Lieutenant Colonel Rossi
- Officers: Captain Moschetti, Lieutenant Mascolo, Lieutenant Zenesini
- Office 1 / B Services: Captain Bagliani, then Major Fabbri Teodorani, finally Captain (Major since 12 March 1945) Bagliani
- Office 1 / C Information: Captain Grumelli, then Lieutenant Colonel Rossi, then Lieutenant Colonel Valli, finally Lieutenant Colonel Cerruti
- Officers: Senior Captain Colombini, Lieutenant Mazzucchelli
- Office 2 / A Staff: Captain Piazza

---

1 In the drafting of the staff, the grades of the officers and non-commissioned officers were reported as indicated by Pieramedeo Baldrati in his monumental monograph on the Great Unit "San Marco… San Marco - History of a Division" (work cited in the bibliography). The correspondence of the degrees adopted by Baldrati is the following:
- Soldier = Marò
- Chosen Soldier = Chosen
- Corporal  = Infantry Corporal of the Navy
- Caporalmaggiore = Deputy Chief
- Sergeant  = Sergeant
- Sergeant Major = Second Chief
- Ordinary Marshal = Head of 3rd Class
- Chief Marshal = 2nd Class Chief
- Marshal Major = Head of 1st Class
- Assistant Marshal = Assistant
- Aspirant = Ensign or Aspirant
- Lieutenant = Corvette Lieutenant
- Lieutenant = Frigate Lieutenant
- Captain = Vessel Lieutenant
- Major =  Corvette Captain
- Lieutenant Colonel = Frigate Captain
- Colonel = Vessel Captain

- Officers: Captain Togni, Lieutenant Romani, Lieutenant M. Adriani, Lieutenant Bellotto
- Office 2 / B Personnel: Lieutenant Giovanninetti
- Office 3 / A Justice: Lieutenant Colonel Tinebra, later Captain Regis
- Prison: Lieutenant Valli
- Divisional Court: Lieutenant Colonel Palma
- Office 3 / B Prisoners: Captain Colombini junior
- Office 4 / A Intendency: Lieutenant Colonel Nolli, then Lieutenant Colonel Durante, then Captain Bagliani, subsequently Lieutenant I.G.S. Taddeucci, and finally Lieutenant Colonel Guardigli
- Office 4 / B Healthcare: Major Rippa doctor
- Officers: Medical Captain Coletti, Medical Captain Schivi
- Office 4 / C Veterinary: Lieutenant Colonel Pirani, then Major Romano
- Officers: Lieutenant Pessa
- Office 4 / D Spiritual Assistance: Captain Father De Marchi, Lieutenant Don Carlino
- Office 5 Transport: Lieutenant Zenesini, then Captain Arcangeli, then Captain Casini, finally Lieutenant Priorelli
- Divisional Depot (BS): Lieutenant Colonel G.N. Gypsies
- Officers: Lieutenant of Vascello Jovacchini, Captain Buzzi, Lieutenant Alvino, Lieutenant Viale, Lieutenant Virgilio, Lieutenant Brunelli, Lieutenant Dalla Torre, Lieutenant Ferro, Lieutenant Mazzoldi, Lieutenant Premoli
- Marine Infantry Depot: Captain of Corvetta Navone, then Captain of Corvetta Foldi, finally 1st Captain Pessi
- Interpreters Office: Captain Palea, Captain Martinozzi, Lieutenant Tomini, Lieutenant Weber, Lieutenant Tomini, Lieutenant Berger
- UDOF (Fascist Orientation Office): Lieutenant Colonel Cerruti
- 3rd Company G.N.R. Railway - Commander: Captain Petri
- 3rd Company G.N.R. Road - Commander: Captain Tarquini
- 3rd Military Police Section - Commander: Lieutenant Sanna
- 10th Military Police Section - Commander: Captain Bonapace
- D.K.V. n. 182: Brigade General Von Alberti, then Brigade General Hildebrandt

## 5th Marine Infantry Regiment
- Regimental Command Company
- Light Infantry Column
- I Battalion
- II Battalion
- III Battalion
- 105th Tank Destroyer Company

## 6th Marine Infantry Regiment
- Regimental Command Company
- Light Infantry Column
- I Battalion
- II Battalion
- III Battalion
- 106th Tank Destroyer Company

## 3rd Artillery Regiment
- Regimental Command Battery
- Light column
- I Donned 75/13 Group
- II Hippotrained 100/17 Group
- III Hippotrained 100/17 Group
- IV Mechanical Towing 149/19 Group

## III Exploring Group (Arditi)
- Command Department
- 1st Light Squadron
- 2nd Light Squadron
- 3rd Heavy Squadron
- Special Squadron (Complements) - *dissolved on February 15, 1945*

## Divisional Units
- III Pioneers Battalion:
    - Command Company
    - 1st Company
    - 2nd Company
    - 3rd Company
- III Transmissions Battalion:
    - Command Company
    - 1st Company
    - 2nd Company
    - 3rd Company
- III Transport Battalion:
    - Command Company
    - 3 transport columns
    - 3rd Truck Company
    - 3rd Company Workshop
    - 3rd Supply Company
- CIII Complements Battalion, dissolved on 09/20/44
- 3rd Company Hunters Carro
- Health Department:
    - 3rd Healthcare Company
    - 103rd Healthcare Company
    - I Surgical Nucleus
    - II Surgical Nucleus
    - III Ambulance Platoon
    - Recovery Service and Fallen Honors
- III Supply Group:
    - Command Company
    - 3rd Company Administration
    - 3rd Company Butchers
    - 3rd Panettieri Company
- 3rd Subsistence Company
- 3rd Veterinary Company

- 3rd Military Police Section 10th Military Police Section
- Collection Battalion (stragglers and rebels), established on 12/16/44
- Military Court - Military Prison
- Marine Infantry Depot and Divisional Depot
- Divisional Musical Band

## Departments reporting directly to the Division
- Armed Train
- I Coastal Post Artillery Group:
  - 1st Battery 75/27
  - 2nd Battery 90/53
  - 3rd Battery 149/19
  - 4th Battery 149/19
- III Coastal Post Artillery Group:
  - 7th Battery 75/27
  - 8th Battery 100/17
- Armored Pontoon G.M. 194 ex "Faà di Bruno", belonging to the Republican National Navy, but inserted in the coastal defense of Savona under the jurisdiction of "San Marco", armed with 2 381/45 guns, 4 76/40 anti-aircraft guns and some 20 machine guns mm.
- Savona Defense Command

## Staff
Situation as of 5 September 1944:

|  | Expected | Present |
|---|---|---|
| Officers | 720 | 606 |
| Non-commissioned officers | 1,528 | 1,206 |
| Troop | 14,197 | 11,012 |
| TOTAL | 16,445 | 12,824 |

The staff of the Division as of January 1, 1945 amounts to[2]:
Officers = 508
Non-commissioned officers = 1.073
Troop = 7.172
TOTAL = 8,753

At the end of April 1945, the soldiers in service at "San Marco" who surrendered to the Allied forces and the partisans can be traced back to about 9,000.

## Weapons
- Breda submachine guns 30 = 148
- Breda / MG 42 machine guns = 226
- Heavy machine gunner 20 mm = 37
- Mortars 80 mm = 90
- Accompaniment guns = 12
- Heavy guns model 38 = 3
- Pak counter tank guns 40 = 22
- Mountain howitzers 75/13 = 12
- 75/27 guns model 11 = 22
- Howitzers 100/17 model 14 = 24
- Howitzers 149/19 = 12

---

[2] The departments of G.N.R. and the 2nd Battalion of the 6th Regiment engaged in Garfagnana are not included.

As individual armament: Mauser 98K rifle, MAB 38A, Gewehr 41, Walther P38 and Luger 08 pistols, Panzerfaust. In Germany the military were also instructed to use the Sturmgewehr 44, not supplied, even if theoretically 24 are assigned.

## Vehicles
Situation as of 5 September 1944:

|  | Expected | Present |
|---|---|---|
| Large wagons | 490 | 295 |
| Small wagons | 370 | 278 |
| Mobile kitchens | 120 | 110 |
| Carts | 1,210 | 980 |
| Cars | 164 | 60 |
| Motorcycles | 186 | 10 |
| Trucks | 264 | 103 |
| Tractors | 54 | 18 |
| Trailers | 13 | 3 |
| Bus | 12 | 2 |
| Ambulances | 6 | 6 |
| Quadrupeds | 5,370 | 3,010 |

Situation as of January 1, 1945 (the 2$^{nd}$ Battalion of the 6$^{th}$ Regiment is not counted)
- Horses = 1.251
- Vehicles = 240
- Charriots = 518

## Losses of the "San Marco" Division
The ascertained losses of the "San Marco" Division amount to 803 known fallen, 497 unknown fallen, 564 missing, 759 wounded.

## 5$^{th}$ Marine Infantry Regiment
Back in Italy, on 7 August the 5$^{th}$ Marine Infantry Regiment was deployed in Quiliano with the Regimental Command Company, while the 105$^{th}$ Carro Destroyer Company was headquartered in Savona, with the task of contributing to the defense of the III Sector, excluded from Celle Ligure at Capo Vado, in competition with the III Battalion. The III Sector was one of the few where it was possible to make an enemy landing, in Vado and Savona there were also many accesses to Piedmont. On 20 September the Command of the 5$^{th}$ Regiment and the Regimental Command Company moved to Forte Tagliata del Giovo. In mid-October, in connection with the transfer to the Gothic line of the 2$^{nd}$ Battalion of the 6$^{th}$ Regiment, the 5$^{th}$ Regiment ordered continuous reconnaissance to cover the movement. On 30 October he carried out an extensive reconnaissance which, connecting with the Meinholdt Group on the Turchino, went as far as Urbe, with small clashes with groups of partisans, in the late evening the departments returned to their starting bases. Between 28 and 30 November another operation was carried out on the watershed of the Passo del Faiallo, with the capture of numerous partisans. Another reconnaissance in force was carried out by the whole Regiment on 9 December, meeting little resistance. As of 1$^{st}$ January 1945, the Regiment, with the Regimental Command Company and the 105$^{th}$ Carro Destroyer Company, was headquartered at Forte Tagliata del Giovo. On 27 February the Command with its Departments carried out a roundup between Olbicella - Pian Castagna - Urbe - Martina - Orba - Piampaludo, with the capture of numerous partisans and the recovery of numerous weapons. On 11 March, Marshal Graziani

was present, the Regimental Command Company and the 105th Carro Destroyer Company carried out a fire maneuver at Sassello. On 25 April the Command began its withdrawal on Acqui with the 105th Company Destroyers Carro, minus the Company Command Regimental which, due to the defection of its commander, was captured by the partisans. On the 26th the Command, with a share of the Light Column and the 105th Company Destroyers Carro, reached Acqui and then continued on Alessandria and reached Valenza, crossed the Po and stopped. On the 27th the departments continued their retreat, passing Mortara and moving to Vigevano, which was passed on the 28th. On the 29th, the Commander of the Regiment, Colonel Sordi, took command of all the Departments of the "San Marco" that had crossed the Ticino. The retreat of the Departments continued towards Abbiategrasso. Arrived in Magenta on the 30th, the 5th Regiment surrendered itself as a prisoner of war in the evening.

## Organization chart

- Commander: Colonel Alberto Seraglia, then Colonel Giuseppe Sordi
- Deputy Commander: Lieutenant Colonel Alfredo Cantella
- Adjutant Major: Lieutenant Vettorato, then Major Valenti
- Office 1 / B Services: Captain Caldati
- Office 1 / C Information: Lieutenant Costanza
- Office 4 / A Intendency: Lieutenant Minelli
- Office 4 / C Veterinary: Lieutenant Doctor Valcalopulo
- Office 4 / D Spiritual Assistance: Lieutenant Father Bartolini
- Regimental Command Company - Commander: Captain Baricelli, subsequently Lieutenant De Lucia, then Captain Raimondi and finally Lieutenant Giorgi. Officers: Lieutenant Bernabò, Lieutenant Caristia, Lieutenant Coletti, Lieutenant Gasperotti, Lieutenant Innocenti, Lieutenant Morabiti, Lieutenant Crupi, Lieutenant Ricciardi, Lieutenant Scrollavezza, Lieutenant Sermenghi, Lieutenant Sesta, Lieutenant Simonetti
- Light Infantry Column - Commander: Captain Ottaviani, then Lieutenant Prato and finally Lieutenant Colonel Mariani. Officers: Lieutenant Busca, Lieutenant De Luca, Lieutenant Lelio, Lieutenant D'Onofrio, Lieutenant Pennesini
- 105th Tank Destroyers Company - Commander: Captain Vettorato, then Lieutenant Capone. Officers: Lieutenant Alborghetti, Lieutenant Bernardi, Lieutenant Santoro, Lieutenant Amato

## 1st Battalion

Returning to Italy at the end of July, he was deployed in defense of the II Sector from Cogoleto excluded to Celle Ligure included, with the task of defending the Apennine access routes of the Colle del Giovo, some of which rolling stock in good condition, for a total of 12 kilometers of the sea front. At the first light of 1 October, the Battalion took part in the operation aimed at eliminating the partisan landing field of Vesime, the occupation of Cortemilia and the complete control of the Apennine watershed from the Passo del Faiallo. In collaboration with the II Battalion, he reached the objectives set on the evening of the 3rd, remaining in place until the 5th, when he returned to the starting positions. From 14 to 22 November the 5th Company carried out a cycle of operations in the Ceva area with the task of cleaning up the area from the partisans. From 28 to 30 November he participated in the sweeping operation on the watershed of the Passo del Faiallo. As of January 1, 1945, the Battalion was headquartered in Stella, with a force of 23 officers, 62 non-commissioned officers and 490 graduates and troops. On 19 April the Battalion assumed the following position of the departments: Command Stella San Martino, 1st Company in Sassello, 2nd in Madonna del Salto, 3rd in Ellera, 4th decentralized, 5th in Corona. On 25 April the Battalion, gathered in Madonna del

Salto, headed towards Sassello where it settled for the night. On the 26th he left Sassello to head for Acqui, reached late in the evening without incident. On the 27th the retreat towards Alexandria continued slowly. On the 28th he continued his movement heading towards Valenza, where he crossed the Po, moving towards Mede. On the 29th the Battalion continued the movement with the Regiment. The 1st Battalion, following the fate of the Regiment, delivered himself as a prisoner on the evening of the 30th in Magenta.

## Organization chart
- Commander: Major Manzi, later Corvette Captain Renato Ferrini, then Lieutenant Aurelio Azzariti, Captain Fazio, Major Antonio Zocchi, finally Lieutenant Colonel Alfredo Cantella
- Adjutant Major: Lieutenant Poletti
- Officers: Lieutenant Alajmo, Medical Lieutenant Pascucci
- Company Command - Commander: Captain Fazio. Officers: Lieutenant Carbone, Lieutenant Costanza, Lieutenant Pompili
- 1st Company - Commander: Lieutenant of Frigate Valastro, later Captain Pozzoli. Officers: Lieutenant Giampolini, Lieutenant Meschini, Lieutenant Moletti, Lieutenant Anghileri, Lieutenant Caruso, Lieutenant Grenzi, Lieutenant Nascenzi, Lieutenant Perfumo, Lieutenant Somma, Lieutenant Sommi
- 2nd Company - Commander: Lieutenant Bernabò, later Captain Giudi and then Lieutenant Giusti. Officers: Lieutenant Valastro, Lieutenant Alajmo, Lieutenant Garlandi, Lieutenant Gironi, Lieutenant Masini, Lieutenant Monino, Lieutenant Morleschi, Lieutenant Saglimbene, Lieutenant Sarconcelli
- 3rd Company - Commander: Lieutenant of Fregata Nugoli, then Lieutenant of Fregata Monis and finally Lieutenant of Vascello Orco. Officers: Lieutenant Innocenzi, Lieutenant Chirico, Lieutenant Consolani, Lieutenant Jannelli, Lieutenant Luciani
- 4th Company - Commander: Captain Chinari, then Captain Suardi. Officers: Lieutenant Bertani, Lieutenant Jesse, Lieutenant Salimbene, Lieutenant Zavaglia
- 5th Company - Commander: Lieutenant of Corvetta Monticelli, then Captain Spinacci. Officers: Lieutenant Cantoni, Lieutenant Bartel, Lieutenant Cusumano, Lieutenant Minelli.

## Area of employment
Deployed in the area of Genoa, it took on the defense of the second sector from Cogoleto to Celle Ligure, with functions of anti-landing defense and anti-partisan garrison. He set up resistance posts in Il Pero, Sanda, Monte Cucco, Marmorassi, Case Ciatti; to the bitter end defense of the Colle del Giovo.

## 2nd Battalion
Returning to Italy at the end of July, it was deployed in defense of Sector I from Arenzano to Cogoleto inclusive, with the task of defending the Apennine access routes of the Turchino Pass and the Faiallo Pass, for a total of 12 kilometers of the sea front. On 1 October the Battalion took part in the operation aimed at eliminating the partisan landing field of Vesime, the occupation of Cortemilia and the complete control of the Apennine watershed from the Passo del Faiallo. In collaboration with the 1st Battalion, he reached the objectives set on the evening of the 3rd, without encountering great resistance from the partisan, remaining in place until the 5th, when he returned to the starting positions. On November 16 the Battalion carried out a roundup in the area between Montenotte Inferiore and Montenotte Superiore, capturing numerous partisans and destroying shelters and deposits. As of January 1, 1945, the Battalion was headquartered in Stella, with a force of 21 officers, 62 non-commissioned officers and 539 graduates and troops. On 27 February the Battalion carried out a roundup between Olbicella-Pian chestnut-Urbe-Martina-Orba-Piampaludo, with firefights

and the capture of numerous partisans, as well as the recovery of numerous weapons. On April 25, the Battalion began retreating from the coast towards the hinterland, minus the 8th Company which, thanks to the defection of the commander, is considered lost, apart from a few elements who manage to reach the Battalion. On the 26th he followed the movement of the 1st Battalion and reached Acqui in the night. On the 27th the retreat towards Alexandria continued slowly. On the 28th the movement continued heading towards Valenza, where it crosses the Po, moving towards Mede, following the 1st Battalion. On the 29th the Battalion continued the movement with the Regiment. The II Battalion, following the fate of the Regiment, delivered himself prisoner on the evening of the 30th in Magenta.

## Organization chart
- Commander: Major Giuseppe Santoro, then Major Mario Federico Nasso
- Adjutant Major: Lieutenant Crespi, then Lieutenant Vettorato and finally Lieutenant Sirola
- Officers: Lieutenant La Galla, Sergeant A.U. Bianchini
- Command Company: Lieutenant Bertucci
- 6th Company - Commander: Officers - Lieutenant Aureli, then Lieutenant Gualtieri
- 7th Company - Commander: Lieutenant Dragotti, then Lieutenant Busca. Officers: Lieutenant Di Martino, Lieutenant Guidoreni, Lieutenant Colacchioni Gualtieri, Lieutenant Morlaschi, Lieutenant Zangiacomi
- 8th Company - Commander: Captain Bastari, then Lieutenant Lombardi. Officers: Lieutenant Bertucci, Lieutenant Consolini, Lieutenant Parravicini, Lieutenant Restelli, Lieutenant Vitiello
- 9th Company - Commander: Lieutenant Orlando, then Lieutenant Mammuccari and finally Captain Bastari. Officers: Lieutenant Fabiano, Lieutenant Fiori, Lieutenant Nicastro, Lieutenant Scrofina
- 10th Company - Commander: Lieutenant of Corvetta Fabiano. Officers: Lieutenant Lombardi, Lieutenant Ronchetti

## Area of employment
Deployed in the Genoa area, it took on the defense of the 1st sector from Arenzano to Cogoleto inclusive, with anti-landing defense and anti-partisan defense functions. He set up resistance posts at Bric del Dente, Passo del Faiallo, Sciarborasca; indefinite defense of the Passo del Faiallo.

## 3rd Battalion
Returning to Italy at the end of July, he was deployed to Savona, assuming with the Command of the 5th Navy Infantry Regiment and the 105th Tank Destroyer Company, the defense of the III sector from Celle to Capo Vado, with anti-landing defense and security functions. of the communication routes to the Apennine watershed. During the early October operations involving the valleys of the Apennine watershed, the Battalion remained the only Department, together with the artillerymen, deployed on the coast. On Christmas Eve the Battalion Command was ordered to prepare to move within 48 hours to an unknown destination. The centralization orders were issued to the Companies and provisions were made to reschedule. On 27 December 1944 the Battalion began the transfer to Emilia-Romagna divided into two rates: the truck-mounted troops along the Genoa - Voghera - Piacenza - Modena - Abetone route, the horse-drawn carriage along the Genoa - La Spezia - Pievepelago - Abetone route . While the transfer of the troops was carried out using coaches supplied by the Army Command, the transfer of the carriage column was more complex, due to the lack of suitable quadrupeds. When it reached Ponte dell'Olio, contrary to what was initially

established, the Battalion was assigned to depend on the 162$^{nd}$ Infanterie-Division and employed, in anti-partisan operations, in the area from the province of Piacenza to the immediate rear of the front line. On January 16, 1945 he left Ponte dell'Olio, aboard a column on a Fiat 626, and, along the Piacenza-SS 9-Ponte Taro-Modena-SS 12 route, he reached Maranello on the 18$^{th}$, where he had to leave, due to the lack of vehicles, almost all the personal and departmental material, starting off on foot with destination Pievepelago, reached on the 22$^{nd}$. Pallerone-Monzone-Vigneto-Gragnana-Pontecosi-Cerageto-Passo delle Radici-Corfino-Sant'Anna-Fiumalbo. On the 24$^{th}$ the Battalion took over the defense of the sector, under the responsibility of the 232$^{nd}$ Infanterie-Division, giving the change to the III Regiment of the 263$^{rd}$ Infanterie-Division. The Battalion Command was placed in Abetone, with the Companies deployed between Alpe Tre Potenze-Pianosinatico-Monte Maggiore-Libro Aperto. The line consisted of underground bunkers, protected by tree trunks and covered with a strong layer of earth, resistant to mortar and medium-caliber artillery, defended by mined anti-personnel and anti-tank tracts and barbed wire barrages. The carriage came online only on February 12, after having traveled through roads and passes covered with snow and ice, which caused the loss of horses and wagons, and sustained firefights with partisans. On January 29, the Americans attacked the Pianosinatico area where they conquered the Casermetta di Rimessa, which was recaptured the following day, and on the 30$^{th}$ the positions defended by the 11$^{th}$ Company. The attack was repulsed with heavy losses from the attackers. On the front, patrols continued in no man's land and American artillery and mortar fire was systematic. Furthermore, only on cloudy days there was no enemy air activity. With the arrival of the carriage column in Pievepelago, it was finally possible to proceed with the distribution of the material from the house to the marines, in addition to reinforcing the personnel of the departments in line with the return of the marines of the escort to the belonging companies. The months of February and March passed without significant actions, except for the continuous patrol activity, even during the day, and the daily bombings, even with phosphorus bombs, by the Americans. On 25 March, some officers and non-commissioned officers and 30 marines as complements arrived at the Battalion from the "San Marco" Stage Command in Milan, who were immediately assigned and sent to the online companies. The month of April began with the usual activity of patrols, although the preparations for the final offensive were evident, materialized with an increase in the bombing of enemy artillery and the acquired presence of armored and armored vehicles. On April 17, the Battalion Command sent the companies the order to retreat to begin the evening of the following day. On the 18$^{th}$ the Americans unleashed a violent attack on the positions defended by the 15$^{th}$ Company in Pianosinatico, considering them already evacuated. The reaction of the marines was violent and forced the enemy to retreat with heavy losses. Heavy losses also among the marines. On the evening of the 18$^{th}$, the Companies gathered in Abetone and began the retreat. on the 19$^{th}$ the Battalion passed Pievepelago to Pavullo, on the 21$^{st}$ it entered Maranello reaching Reggio Emilia on the 22$^{nd}$. On the 23$^{rd}$ he headed towards Parma, which he passed towards Tre Casali, where, after having suffered an attack by American armored forces together with partisan elements, he stopped for the night. The Battalion Command released all the native or resident marines in Emilia, so that the force dropped to just over 300 units. On the 24$^{th}$ he set out towards the Po, passing it and reaching Roccabianca, then he reached Polesine Parmense. On April 26, 1945 at 8 am the III Battalion of the 5$^{th}$ Regiment of Navy Infantry ceased to exist.

## Organization chart
- Commander: Major Enrico Modonesi, then Major Giovanni Blotto, then Captain Brunetti, Captain Lucio Sestito, finally Captain Carlo Manzotti
- Adjutant Major: Lieutenant Sirola
- Officers: Lieutenant Silvestri, Lieutenant De Luise, Lieutenant Baron, Lieutenant Medical Taini

- Company Command: Lieutenant of Corvetta Lapomarda. Officers: Second Lieutenant Di Giorgio
- 11th Company - Commander: Lieutenant Dosi. Officers: Lieutenant Degano; Lieutenant Bagnaresi, Lieutenant Callicchio, Lieutenant Copes, Lieutenant Dini, Lieutenant Pellegrino, Lieutenant Serpi, Sergeant I.G.S. Protasio Meles
- 12th Company - Commander: Lieutenant of Fregata Alvino, then Lieutenant Busca, finally Lieutenant Lorenzoni. Officers: Lieutenant Borroni, Lieutenant Basile, Lieutenant Bertucci, Lieutenant Bianchetti, Lieutenant Bonomini, Lieutenant Dosi, Lieutenant Salvo, Lieutenant Lorenzoni
- 13th Company - Commander: Captain Manzotti, then Lieutenant Osca. Officers: Lieutenant Busca, Lieutenant Gamacchio, Lieutenant Danti, Lieutenant Diamanti, Lieutenant Noah, Lieutenant Oggero, Lieutenant Viale, Aspirant Benini
- 14th Company - Commander: Captain Brunetti. Officers: Lieutenant Boroni, Lieutenant Danti, Lieutenant Nicastro, Lieutenant Bellini, Lieutenant Carlandrea Pellegrino, Lieutenant Poli-Capuci
- 15th Company - Commander: Lieutenant of Corvetta Lapomarda, then Captain Sestito. Officers: Lieutenant Biamonti, Lieutenant Bertucci, Lieutenant Cutrì, Lieutenant Reni

## Area of employment

Deployed in the Savona area, he took on the defense of the sector from Celle Ligure to Capo Vado, with anti-landing defense functions and anti-partisan garrison in the rear of the Battalion. Transferred to the southern front, along the way he carried out anti-partisan operations in the province of Piacenza. Once in line on Abetone, he placed the Command in Abetone, deploying the 13th Company in Alpe Tre Potenze, the 11th in Pianosinatico, the 14th in Monte Maggiore-Libro Aperto, the 12th in reserve, the 15th decentralized, the Logistics Base and the Carreggio in Pievepelago.

## 6th Marine Infantry Regiment

Back in Italy, on 7 August the 6th Marine Infantry Regiment was deployed in Ortovero, while the Regimental Command Company and the 106th Carro Destroyer Company took up positions in Albenga. On 6 October the Command moved to Calice Ligure. In mid-October, in relation to the transfer to the Gothic line of the 2nd Battalion of the 6th, the Regiment ordered continuous reconnaissance to cover the movement. On October 30, with three columns, he carried out an extensive reconnaissance that enveloped the Colle del Melogno, with small clashes with groups of partisans, in the late evening the departments returned to their starting bases. On 25 April the Command, the Regimental Command Company and the Light Column remained in their positions, while the 106th Carro Destroyer Company began the movement towards Acqui. On the 26th all the other departments also began the movement towards Acqui, which they reached on the 27th, where they stopped, except the Light Column which continued towards Alexandria. On the 28th the Command, the Regimental Command Company and the 106th Carro Destroyer Company, after reaching Alessandria, continued their retreat towards Valmadonna, while the Light Column stopped in Alessandria. On the 29th the Regimental Departments delivered themselves into captivity at the Citadel of Alexandria. Aliquots of the Regiment followed the fate of the 5th Regiment, surrendering their arms on the evening of 30 in Magenta.

## Organization chart

- Commander: Lieutenant Colonel Cristoforo Palma, then Captain Gaetano Tortora, finally Colonel Cesare Chiari
- Adjutant Major: Major Boccaletti, then Captain Battistella, finally Major Azzariti
- Officers: Major Teodorani-Fabbri, Major Zocchi, Captain Paggiarino, Captain Senetiner

- Office 1 / A Operations: Lieutenant Tamburini
- Office 1 / B Services: Captain Paini
- Office 1 / C Information: Lieutenant Peroni
- Office 4 / A Intendency: Lieutenant Minelli
- Office 4 / B Health: Medical Captain Anastasi, then Medical Captain Rago
- Regimental Command Company: Lieutenant I.G.S. Martinazzoli, then the Lieutenant of Corvetta Del Bianco. Officers: Lieutenant Scarambone, Lieutenant Caronni, Lieutenant Crovatto, Lieutenant Del Bianco, Lieutenant Matrobuono, Lieutenant Spinelli
- Light Infantry Column: Lieutenant Zangiacomi, then Captain Massa. Officers: Lieutenant Poli
- 106th Company Destroyers Carro: Captain Battistella, then Captain Capogrossi. Officers: Lieutenant Marcheselli, Lieutenant D'Alfonso, Lieutenant Ficorilli

## 1st Battalion

Returning to Italy at the end of July, it was deployed to defend the IV Sector from Capo Vado excluded to Loano Marina inclusive, with the task of defending the Apennine access routes of Colle del Melogno and the numerous beaches accessible for enemy landings, for a total of 18 km of the sea front. At the first light of 1 October, the Battalion took part in the operation aimed at the complete control of the Apennine watershed from Monte Alto except Giustenice, occupying the Melogno Pass, Osiglia and freeing access to Calizzano. After having conquered Monte Alto, in collaboration with the III Battalion, he took possession of the Colle del Melogno on the evening of the 3rd, after having sustained heavy clashes with the partisans attested in the old fortifications. Having reached the objectives, the Battalion remained in place until 5, when it returned to the starting positions. On October 30, the 3rd company participated in an extensive reconnaissance that from Finale Ligure, through Portio - Orco Feglino - Carbuta - Pian dei Corsi, reached Madonna della Neve, where it connected to the 4th Company which, starting from Pietra Ligure, reached at the Colle del Melogno. During the night the departments returned to Finale Ligure. As of January 1, 1945, the Battalion had a staff of 27 officers, 55 non-commissioned officers and 534 between graduates and troops. On April 25th the Battalion began to withdraw towards Acqui, continuing its movement on the 26th. Once in Acqui the Battalion continued towards Alessandria on the 27th. On the 28th the Battalion passed Alessandria and reached Valenza where it stopped waiting to cross the Po. The Battalion surrendered in captivity at the Citadel of Alexandria.

## Organization chart

- Commander: Captain Tullio Mozzone, then Captain Enrico Paggiarino, finally Lieutenant Colonel Guido Falconi
- Officers: Lieutenant Pfeiffer
- Company Command - Commander:? . Officers: Lieutenant Faraone, Lieutenant Soave
- 1st Company - Commander: Lieutenant of Vascello Basiaco, then Captain Bergonzi. Officers: Lieutenant Dondi; Second Lieutenant Mazzoldi, Second Lieutenant Mercuri
- 2nd Company - Commander: Lieutenant Danon. Officers: Lieutenant Faraboschi, Lieutenant Pierleoni, Lieutenant Calisi, Lieutenant De Lucis, Lieutenant Magni, Aspirant Alberti
- 3rd Company - Commander: Lieutenant Faraone, then Lieutenant Manzelli. Officers: Lieutenant Brandani, Lieutenant Casonato, Lieutenant Filacchione
- 4th Company - Commander: Lieutenant Bertoli, then Captain Paggiarino. Officers: Lieutenant Tiraboschi, Lieutenant Cartaino, Lieutenant Caristia, Lieutenant Nava
- 5th Company - Commander: Captain Gregori. Officers: Lieutenant Magni, Lieutenant Frassa, Lieutenant Rolando, Lieutenant Occhini, Lieutenant Staffieri

## Area of employment

Deployed in the Savona area, it took on the defense of the fourth sector from Capo Vado to Loano Marina included, with anti-landing defense and anti-partisan garrison functions. He set up resistance posts in Monte Alto, San Giorgio, Vezzi Portio, Orco Feglino, Calice Ligure; to the bitter end defense of the Melogno hill.

## 2nd Battalion

Returning to Italy at the end of July, it was initially deployed in the Andora area in August, and in September he took over the defense of the sixth sector from Capo Santa Croce to Capo Cervo. He participated in the elimination of the Vesime landing field and in the occupation of Cortemilia with the 3rd Exploring Group from 1 to 5 October. On October 15, the Division Command gave the order to the Bird Commander to prepare the Battalion "Within 72 hours" to leave for the southern front. Orders were issued to the Companies to immediately reach Cairo Montenotte, where the armaments and clothing were reintegrated , as well as receiving 50 complements to complete the staff. Due to the difficulty of transport, the concentration of the Battalion lasted for a few days, so that only on October 20 could the transfer to the Garfagnana front, divided into three stages of march, begin. The transfer was carried out partly on foot, partly by truck and partly by rail, along the route Celle Ligure - Genoa - La Spezia - Aulla - Camporgiano - Castelnuovo Garfagnana[3]. The last part of the journey was carried out with trucks belonging to the IV Transport Battalion of the "Monterosa" Division. The Battalion was operationally placed under the control of the "Schirowsky" Combat Group, while administratively it was under the control of the 1st Alpine Regiment Command of the 4th "Monterosa" Division. On 29 October 1944 the Battalion entered the line replacing the IB Battalion of the 285th Germanic Regiment, assuming the defense of the sector located between Le Rocchette, in connection with the "Intra" Alpini Battalion, and the furrow between Taverna and Fiattone, in connection with the "Brescia" Alpini Battalion. It was the western subsector of the Serchio. The defensive line consisted of holes for isolated shooters, trench sections, group shelters, command posts; the passive defenses by fences and some minefields in front of the positions of the 6th and 8th Company. After a few days, spent reinforcing the defenses and laying the connections between the Command and the line posts, patrol activities began. In front of him he found first the Brazilians of the FEB and then the Americans of the 92nd Division. In early November, the first actions of the enemy patrols against the marines' positions began. On November 16 a strong attack was launched against the positions defended by the 7th and 9th Company, which allowed the Americans to occupy top 1029, top 1031, altitude 832 and the collar. During the night German and Italian reinforcements arrived, which allowed at dawn to counterattack and regain some quotas. On the 19th the situation had returned to the initial one, all the positions initially lost had been reoccupied and the defensive line was stabilized. On 20 November the II Battalion passed operationally under the command of the 1st Alpine Regiment. On this line it successfully sustained further defensive combat, against patrols and attacks by the force of a Company, in November and December, as well as carrying out continuous exploratory patrols within no man's land. To underline the constant shelling by the Allied artillery and the raids by fighter-bombers, which resulted in deaths and injuries. He took part in the "Wintergewitter" offensive of Christmas 1944 as part of the 1st attack column, which struck Vergemoli and Gallicano, pushing beyond the Turrite di Gallicano in the Serchio furrow to Bolognana, reached in the morning of the 28th. The positive result of the offensive it allowed the Battalion to move the defensive line further south by over two kilometers, placing it on dominant ridges that allowed for better defense. In January 1945 the Battalion departments continued patrolling, as well as repelling some attacks, by the strength of a Company, launched alternately against the positions of Monte

---

3 The II Platoon of the 7th Company, which at the date of the transfer of the Battalion was located in Dego, left late, arriving in Castelnuovo Garfagnana only on October 30, after countless ups and downs due to the scarcity of means of transport and the error of route due to the German liaison non-commissioned officer in charge of accompanying the Platoon.

Faeto, Case Rio, Molazzana, 451 altitude, 437 altitude. 1945 the change in line of the "Monterosa" Departments with the Bersaglieri of the "Italy" Division began, which returned from Germany at the end of 1944. From 1 February the Battalion passed to the operational dependencies of the 1st Bersaglieri Regiment of the "Italia" Division. The alternation between the Alpini of "Monterosa" and the Bersaglieri of "Italy", this always extremely delicate phase, immediately became known to the Americans, who began a series of targeted attacks aimed at verifying the combativeness of the new opponents. In February the marines of the II Battalion had to face, almost daily, not only the American attacks against their positions, but also to contribute with the fire of their weapons to the defense of the positions defended by the Bersaglieri. The main clashes occurred: the 3 in Monte Faeto, the 5 in q. 437, on the 6th in Calomini, on the 8th with the reconquest of q. 437, on the 18th of q. 352, 20 in Case Pozzi, 26 in Monte Faeto, 27 in Calomini, 28 again in Monte Faeto. On the 18th and 19th 5 Officers and 124 among Aspirants, Non-commissioned officers, graduates and troops as complements arrived from Liguria, who were immediately sent in line to reinforce the scarce staff of the Companies. On 2 March the Bersaglieri replaced the marines of the 6th, 7th and 8th Companies in line. On the 6th the order was issued to return to the line and restore the previous tactical dislocations. On the 10th a new attack was unleashed against 437 altitude, defended by the 8th marines, who repelled the attack. On March 13, the Command of the 1st Bersaglieri Regiment communicated to the Battalion Command that, starting from the night, the change with the Bersaglieri began. On March 15 the Battalion began the transfer to La Spezia, carried out partly on foot and partly by rail, with the horse-drawn carriage[4]. Reached La Spezia on the 18th, the Battalion was set aside in a large school building, apart from the 10th Company which had to settle in an abandoned factory, and stayed there until the 25th, participating in the parade of the 23rd on the occasion of the ceremony for the foundation of the Fasci of Combat, and then continue towards Deiva on the 26th. From here the order was received to reach Sestri Levante, where the 30th arrived, by the Command of the 1st Alpine Regiment of the "Monterosa", on which it operationally depended until the end of the hostilities. The tasks entrusted to the Battalion were safety on the SS 1 up to Passo del Bracco and on the SP Sestri-Passo Centocroci from the actions of the partisan bands operating in the area. On 23 April the Battalion Command received the order to withdraw which, through Sestri Levante and Lavagna, brought the Department to Chiavari, where it joined the "Monterosa" Departments. From Chiavari, on the 25th, the column began its retreat towards the Po Valley with the 2nd Battalion of the 6th FM Regiment which always carried out avant-garde functions. After passing Rapallo and the Ruta Pass, the column deviated towards the Scoffera Pass, when it reached Uscio it stopped surrendering to the Americans on 27 April 1945. On that date, the 2nd Battalion of the 6th Regiment of the "San Marco Division ceased to exist.

The Battalion during the operational cycle in Garfagnana and in the Ligurian Riviera di Levante was indicated with the name of Battalion "Uccelli", from the name of its Commander.

**Organization chart Battaglione**
- Commander: Corvette Captain (later Frigate Captain) Luigi Uccelli[5], then Captain Umberto Feriani
- Adjutant Major: Lieutenant Sommaiuolo
- Officers: Lieutenant Orselli, Lieutenant Infante, Lieutenant Natale, Lieutenant Doctor Del Vecchio, Lieutenant Martial Doctor, Captain Burrone, Chaplain Lieutenant don Carreggio
- Command Company: Lieutenant Monteverde. Officers: Lieutenant Ratti, Lieutenant Planted
- 6th Company - Commander: Lieutenant Talamo, then Lieutenant Seht. Officers: Lieutenant

---
4 Due to the chronic shortage of quadrupeds, many carts were pulled with oxen, which further slowed the march..
5 The surrender was not agreed by the Captain of Frigate Uccelli but by Captain Feriani, who had assumed command of the Battalion on the 26th as the Captain of Frigate Birds had gone into hiding because he feared reprisals from the British, who had inflicted on him the death penalty in 1941 in AOI.

Bagnaresi, Lieutenant Carnio, Lieutenant Rolando, Lieutenant Mariani, Lieutenant Villani, Aspirant Magnani
- 7th Company - Commander: Captain Burroni, then Lieutenant Arena. Officers: Lieutenant Talamo, Lieutenant Abriani, Lieutenant Bertini, Lieutenant Capasso, Lieutenant Zamgiacomi; Second Lieutenant Crabs, Second Lieutenant Del Nero
- 8th Company - Commander: Captain Feriani. Officers: Lieutenant Seth, Lieutenant Botti, Lieutenant Gatti, Lieutenant Sara, Lieutenant Agostini, Lieutenant Le Rose, Lieutenant Martinola, Lieutenant Marzon
- 9th Company - Commander: Captain Bergonzi, then Lieutenant De Carli. Officers: Lieutenant Calcaterra, Lieutenant Belardinelli, Lieutenant Tordi, Lieutenant Maiorana, Aspirant Jaccarelli
- 10th Company - Commander: Captain Messina. Officers: Lieutenant Di Natale, Lieutenant Costantini, Lieutenant Caronni, Lieutenant Gallisai, Lieutenant Guerra, Lieutenant Marcheselli, Lieutenant Pazzini, Aspirant Pessina

## Area of employment

Initially deployed in the Andora area, in the Riviera di Ponente, it took on the defense of the sector from Capo Santa Croce to Capo Cervo, operated in the Val Bormida and in the Piana di Albenga. Transferred to the Garfagnana front, he placed the Command in Monterotondo, next to the Castelnuovo Garfagnana-Monte Perpoli roadway, and deployed the 6th Company between Le Rocchette - Grottorotondo -south side of Monte d'Anima-Case Foce (included); the 7th between Case Foce (excluded) - Case Croce Sotto - quota 395 (included); the 8th between 395 (excluded) - Cantonbacci-Taverna (included); the 9th decentralized with command post in Eglio; the 10th decentralized with command post in Montaltissimo. The logistic base was located in Castelnuovo Garfagnana and the dressing room in an old chapel between Castelnuovo and Torrite. Following the Christmas offensive, the defensive line was pushed forward by two kilometers, occupying dominant positions (Vergemoli - Calomini - Monte Faeto - altitude 437), which allowed a better defense of the groove of the Turrite di Gallicano. The 6th, 7th, 8th Company were deployed on the new positions, the 9th decentralized for Plotoni to the Rifle Companies, the 10th in a central position. Returning to Liguria, it was deployed in the hinterland of Sestri Levante, with the Command placed in Castiglione Chiavarese, the 6th Company in Bargonasco, the 7th in Velva, the 8th in San Saturnino Comeglio, the 9th at the Bracco Pass, the 10th at Bracco country. This deployment remained in place until April 23 when the retreat towards Sestri Levante began.

## 3rd Battalion

Returning to Italy at the end of July, it was deployed to defend the V Sector from Loano Marina excluded to Capo Santa Chiara excluded, with the task of defending the Apennine access routes of Colle del Melogno and the numerous beaches accessible for enemy landings, for a total of 16 kilometers of the sea front. At 6 am on 1 October, the Battalion took part in the operation aimed at the complete control of the Apennine watershed from Monte Alto excluding Giustenice, occupying the Melogno Pass, Osiglia and freeing access to Calizzano. In collaboration with the 1st Battalion, he took possession of the Colle del Melogno on the evening of the 3rd, after having sustained heavy clashes with the partisans attested in the old fortifications. Having reached the objectives, the Battalion remained in place until 5, when it returned to the starting positions. On October 30, the Battalion participated in an extensive reconnaissance that from Borghetto, through Toirano - Giogo di Toirano - Bardineto - Calizzano, reached Colle del Melogno, where it connected to the two companies of the 1st Battalion of the 6th Regiment. During the night the departments returned to Borghetto. As of January 1, 1945, the Battalion was headquartered in Borgio Verezzi, with a force of 28 officers, 77 non-commissioned officers and 565 between graduates and troops. On February 2, the Battalion's counter-band attacked a partisan camp in Pian dei Corsi by surprise, destroying it. Heavy losses by the partisans and a considerable loot of weapons and recovered material. On 25 April the Battalion moved from Calice Ligure and, crossing Finale Ligure - Spotorno - Vado Ligure - Savona, reached Altare in the night, after having sustained some battles against partisan groups along the coast. During the night, a share of the 15th Company returned to Savona to unlock the 13th Company engaged by strong partisan gangs. After a hard fight, the partisans disappeared and the two companies reached Altare. On the morning of the 26th, the entire Battalion began its movement towards Acqui, reached undisturbed during the day. On the 27th he left Acqui to head towards Alessandria, where he arrived before the 1st Battalion. On the 28th the Battalion passed Alexandria and reached Valenza where it stopped waiting to cross the Po. On the 29th the III Battalion surrendered itself to captivity at the Citadel of Alexandria.

## Organization chart
- Commander: Major Giorgio De Zorzi
- Adjutant Major: Lieutenant Ferraro, then Captain Cardinals
- Officers: Lieutenant Canciello, Lieutenant Fracassi, Lieutenant Facciolo, Lieutenant Damonte, Medical Lieutenant Esposito, Medical Lieutenant De Benedetti, Veterinary Lieutenant Potocco, Lieutenant Annigoni
- Command Company: Captain Modonesi. Officers: Lieutenant D'Angelo, Lieutenant Guadagnini
- 11th Company - Commander: Lieutenant of Vascello Feriani, then Captain Buzzi, finally Captain Capogrossi. Officers: Lieutenant Caselli, Lieutenant Monteverde, Lieutenant Tamburi, Lieutenant Bartoletti, Lieutenant Giorgioni, Lieutenant Guerra, Lieutenant Marianini, Lieutenant Pellegrinetti, Lieutenant Saccaro, Lieutenant Scrollavezza
- 12th Company - Commander: Lieutenant Fabiani (Captain since 1 January 1945). Officers: Lieutenant Ferraro, Lieutenant De Cadilhac, Lieutenant Fracassi, Lieutenant Moro, Russian Lieutenant, Second Lieutenant Scrofina
- 13th Company - Commander: Captain Cardinals, then Lieutenant Martinola. Officers: Second Lieutenant Barabesi, Lieutenant Giorgi, Lieutenant Martinola, Lieutenant Noah, Lieutenant Salerno
- 14th Company - Commander: Captain Gaidondi, then Captain Serrano. Officers: Lieutenant Ferrero, Lieutenant Lucattelli, Lieutenant Mongioi, Lieutenant Pavan, Lieutenant Repetti
- 15th Company - Commander: Captain of Corvetta De Zorzi, then Lieutenant Nerbiato, then Lieutenant Gregori, Captain Serrano, finally Lieutenant Ricci. Officers: Lieutenant Lunardini, Lieutenant Nerbiato, Lieutenant Corino, Lieutenant D'Alfonso.

## Area of employment
Deployed in the Savona area, it took on the defense of the V sector from Loano Marina to Capo Santa Croce, with anti-landing defense and anti-partisan defense functions. He set up resistance posts in Monte Collarino, Bardino Vecchio, San Lorenzo, Salto del Lupo, Balestrino, Salea; to the bitter end defense of Colle del Melogno.

## 3rd Artillery Regiment
Returning to Italy between late July and early August, on 7 August the 3rd Artillery Regiment was deployed in Quiliano with the Regimental Command Battery. On 28 August the 3rd Command was transferred to Altare. As of 1 January 1945, the Regiment was headquartered in Cadibona. On the night of January 31, the batteries of the Regiment carried out retaliatory shots on Roccaverano, Monte Alto, Valle di Cortemilia and Segno. On 25 April the Command with the Regimental Command

Battery set off towards Acqui. When he reached Acqui he headed for Alessandria, stopping on the 26th just outside the town. On the 27th he crossed the Po reaching Lomello, where he stopped. On the 28th the Command with the Regimental Command Battery continued its movement towards Mortara and Vigevano, overcoming the Ticino. On the 29th the Command with the Regimental Command Battery was reunited with the tactical group at the Command of Colonel Sordi and Major Viviani, Commander of the Regiment, assumed command of the rearguard. On the evening of the 30th, after having fulfilled the rearguard task of the Tactical Group, he surrendered himself as a prisoner of war in Magenta.

## Organization chart
- Commander: Lieutenant Colonel Alfredo Possenti, later Colonel Federico Alpaja, then Lieutenant Colonel Angelo Barea-Toscan, Lieutenant Colonel Giuseppe De Martiis, finally Major Francesco Viviani
- Adjutant Major: Captain Landi
- Attendant Officer: Captain Bett, Captain Tei
- Office 1 / A Operations: Captain Merlo
- Office 4 / A Intendency: Second Lieutenant Tabacchini
- Office 4 / B Healthcare: Medical Lieutenant La Medica
- Office 4 / C: Veterinary Veterinary Lieutenant Bugini, later Veterinary Captain Gardelli
- Office 4 / D Spiritual Assistance: Lieutenant Don Giaccone
- Regimental Command Battery - Commander: Second Lieutenant Sioli, then Captain Biglino, then Lieutenant Firmani, finally Lieutenant Bianchi. Officers: Lieutenant De Biase, Lieutenant Trezzi, Lieutenant Moscow

## I Donned 75/13 Group

Returning to Italy in early August 1944, Group I was sent to Sant'Antonio di Ventimiglia under the 34th Infanterie-Division. On 28 August it was located in Dolceacqua, with the batteries positioned in the same location. In support of the Group there was also a 149/19 howitzer of the 11th Battery of the IV Group. He remained employed by the German Division until 5 September 1944, when he returned to the employ of the "San Marco", moving to Millesimo. The Group did not carry out any fire actions, but participated with patrols in contrasting the partisan bands. As of January 1, 1945, the Group was headquartered in Montechiaro Denice, with a force of 20 officers, 44 non-commissioned officers and 539 graduates and troops. From 13 March the I Group was included in the "Valli" Tactical Group, sharing its history until its dissolution.

## Organization chart
- Commander: Captain Silvio Gori
- Adjutant Major: Lieutenant De Conti
- Officers: Lieutenant De Biase, Lieutenant Tabacchini
- Group Command Battery (I) - Commander: Lieutenant Benizzi. Officers: Lieutenant Baroni
- 1st Battery - Commander: Captain Brunetti. Officers: Lieutenant Borreani
- 2nd Battery - Commander: Captain Baranzani, then Lieutenant De Conti. Officers: Second Lieutenant Baucia
- 3rd Battery - Commander: Lieutenant Barbero. Officers: Lieutenant Casciello, Lieutenant Ruzzolini, Lieutenant Vecchietti

## II Hippotrained 100/17 Group

Back in Italy, on 7 August 1944 the II Group was deployed on Monte Ciuto, on the heights of Savona, from where it could control the slope towards Cadibona and the slopes towards Savona and Vado Ligure. From 12 August an Allied air offensive began, lasting a few days, which mainly raged against the newly deployed battery positions. Particularly affected was the 6th Battery, which suffered losses and had considerable skids among its ranks. On the 14th full operation of the Battery was restored, with the return of dozens of stragglers and the arrival of accessories. On 28 August the 4th Battery was deployed in Cima di Prato, the 5th in Verna and the 6th on Monte Ciuto. The Group never carried out fire actions, but participated with patrols in contrasting the partisan bands. As of January 1, 1945, the Group was headquartered in Cadibona, with a force of 20 officers, 56 non-commissioned officers and 295 graduates and troops. On 7 February all the heats of the Group performed control shots with good results. On April 25th the Group set off towards Acqui, where it stopped on the 26th. On the 27th it continued the retreat, reaching Alessandria within the day. On the 28th he moved slowly towards Valmadonna, where he stopped. On the 29th the II Group surrendered itself in captivity at the Citadel of Alexandria.

## Organization chart
- Commander: Captain Ildefonso Secchi
- Adjutant Major: Lieutenant of Vascello Franchi, then Lieutenant Gardelli
- Officers: Lieutenant De Zitti, Lieutenant De Zoff, Second Lieutenant Medical Baroni
- Group Command Battery (II) - Commander: Captain Trippitelli. Officers: Lieutenant Intini, Lieutenant Delle Piane, Lieutenant Verdirosi
- 4th Battery - Commander Captain Giannino, then Captain Angelini. Officers: Lieutenant Perod
- 5th Battery - Commander Captain Carini, later Captain Silva. Officers: Lieutenant Ferrari, Lieutenant Licciardello-Santi, Lieutenant Dell'Orso, Lieutenant De Marinis, Lieutenant Delle Piane
- 6th Battery: Captain Togni. Officers: Lieutenant Bartolomasi, Lieutenant Bozino, Lieutenant Locarni, Lieutenant Pennacchioni, Lieutenant Verdirosi

## III Hippotrained 100/17 Group

Back in Italy, on 7 August 1944 the III Group was deployed in the area of the Sanctuary of Savona, with the batteries positioned on Monte Curlo and Monte Baraccone. The Allied air offensive, unleashed in mid-August and lasted for a few days, raged mainly against the battery posts deployed on the hills around Savona. Particularly affected was the 9th Battery, which suffered losses and had considerable skids among its ranks. On the 14th full operation of the Battery was restored, with the return of dozens of stragglers and the arrival of accessories. As of August 28, the Group Command and all the batteries were deployed in Finale Ligure. In support of the Group there were 3 149/19 howitzers of the 11th Battery of the IV Group. The Group never carried out fire actions, but participated with patrols in contrasting the partisan bands. As of January 1, 1945, the Group was headquartered in Rovieto Stella, with a force of 17 officers, 43 non-commissioned officers and 294 graduates and troops. On 7 February all the heats of the Group performed control shots with good results. On 25 April the Group set off towards Acqui. When he reached Acqui he headed for Alessandria, stopping on the 26th just outside the town. On the 27th he crossed the Po in Valenza and rejoined the Regiment in Lomello. He followed the Regiment beyond the Ticino. On the 29th the Group remained in arms at the disposal of the Regiment. On the evening of the 30th he surrendered himself as a prisoner of war in Magenta.

## Organization chart
- Comandante: Maggiore Renato Andriani
- Aiutante Maggiore: Tenente Salvatori
- Ufficiali: Tenente Forni

- Batteria Comando Gruppo (III) - Comandante: Capitano Betti. Ufficiali: Sottotenente Francia
- 7ª Batteria - Comantante: Tenente Monticelli, poi Capitano Save. Ufficiali: Sottotenente Capovilla, Sottotenente Colacchioni, Sottotenente Dell'Orso
- 8ª Batteria - Comandante: Capitano Angelini. Ufficiali: Tenente Monticelli, Tenente Salvatori, Sottotenente Francia, Sottotenente Lotti, Sottotenente Luchi
- 9ª Batteria - Comandante: Capitano Simoni. Ufficiali: Sottotenente Novi, Sottotenente Ruggeri, Sottotenente Sioli

## IV Mechanical towing unit 149/19guns

Back in Italy, on 7 August 1944 the IV Group was deployed at Altare. On 28 August the Command was deployed in Quiliano, the 10th Battery was in Roviasca and the 12th in Segno, while the howitzers of the 11th Battery were sent to support the I and III Groups. The Group never carried out any fire actions. As of January 1, 1945, the Group had decentralized batteries to support the various sectors, with a force of 14 officers, 41 non-commissioned officers and 294 graduates and troops. On February 7, some heats of the Group carried out control shots with good results. On April 25th the Group set off towards Acqui, where it stopped on the 26th. On the 27th it crossed the Po in Valenza and rejoined the Regiment in Lomello. On the 28th, after having blown up the pieces, he crossed the Po in Valenza and rejoined the Regiment beyond the Ticino. On the 29th the Group remained in arms at the disposal of the Regiment. On the evening of the 30th he surrendered himself as a prisoner of war to Magenta.

## Organization chart
- Commander: Major Ronchi, later Major Francesco Viviani, finally Major Carobulo
- Adjutant Major: Lieutenant De Conti, then Second Lieutenant Avitabile
- Officers: Lieutenant De Biase
- Group Command Battery (IV) - Commander: Captain Silva, later Lieutenant Righetti. Officers: Lieutenant Ankle
- 10th Battery - Commander: Captain Dani. Officers: Lieutenant Gua, Lieutenant Lauro
- 11th Battery - Commander: Captain Corticelli, then Lieutenant Barbrentolo. Officers: Lieutenant Comas, Lieutenant Guarienti
- 12th Battery - Commander: Lieutenant Colonel Ciampolillo. Officers: Lieutenant Lupini, Lieutenant Barbesino

## 3rd Arditi Exploring Group

The 3rd Exploring Group originated from the II Battalion of the X Regiment Arditi "Fiamme Azzurre" which had already fought in Sicily during the Anglo-American landing, and which was reconstituted under the orders of the ancient commander, Major Marcianò, after 8 September 1943. It was the only organic department included in the San Marco, and also the only one that had combat experience. Thanks to the influx of volunteers, careful selection was possible in Germany, which allowed the Department to be one of the few with complete staff, as per the tables, and the complete supply of armaments and vehicles. On March 30, 1944 he was transferred to the Grafenwohr camp and inserted as the 3rd Exploring Group in the Division. Returning to Italy at the end of July 1944, he was immediately employed by the German Command in the Imperia area, where he carried out sweeping and anti-partisan cleaning actions. Faced with the pressing requests to return to the Division's workforce, in early September the Group returned from Imperia, along the road that through Alberga-Bardineto-Calizzano-Millesimo leads to Cairo Montenotte, with the task of moving to Val Bormida and keeping clear the communication routes to Piedmont. During the march he had to endure some firefights with the rebel gangs, always with positive results. Located between Bistagno, Spigno Monferrato and Dego with mobile nuclei between Cairo Montenotte and Acqui / Alessandria, it had numerous clashes with elements of the "Mauri" bands. From 1 to 5 October he participated in the offensive action aimed at clearing the center of Val Bormida and destroying the Vesime landing field, in collaboration with the 2$^{nd}$ Battalion of the 6$^{th}$ Regiment. In the months of October and November he remained at the Division's disposal, continuing to carry out anti-partisan actions. Faced with the pressing requests of the Lombardy Army Command, which wanted to have the Group under its orders, on the orders of Marshal Graziani it was ordered that, starting from 1 December, only the 2$^{nd}$ Squadron would remain under the control of the San Marco, while the rest of the Group would be transferred to Canelli with the task of protecting the Germanic rear. In fact, the entire 3$^{rd}$ Exploring Group was employed in anti-partisan actions under the tactical dependencies of the 34$^{th}$ Infanterie-Division of Von Lieb and only when the retreat of the San Marco from Liguria began, it operated with avant-garde tasks for the benefit of the Departments of the Division to which it belonged, reaching Acqui first, then Alessandria and finally Valenza, where it protected the transit of the Division's comrades. It broke up on the night of May 1$^{st}$ in Magenta.

## Organization chart

- Commander: Lieutenant Colonel Mario Baggiani, then Major Vito Marcianò (Lieutenant Colonel since January 1945)
- Deputy Commander: Captain Romolo Paradisi
- Adjutant Major: Lieutenant Costanzo
- Officers: Lieutenant Silvestri, Lieutenant Icearco, Lieutenant Don Quistilli, Lieutenant Mascolo, Lieutenant Medici Virgilio, Lieutenant Boni, Lieutenant Soliman, Lieutenant Petri, Lieutenant Tanda, Lieutenant Marzullo
- Command Department - Commander: Lieutenant Vincenzo Bonassini. Officers: Lieutenant Francesco Battaglia, Lieutenant Mario Pellegrini
- 1$^{st}$ Light Squadron - Commander: Captain Zanon, later Captain Maffeis, then Captain Azzariti and Captain Cogliavina. Officers: Lieutenant Mangia, Lieutenant Puddinu, Lieutenant Bacchia, Lieutenant Straw Burner, Lieutenant Mascia, Lieutenant Rocchetti, Lieutenant Volpi
- 2$^{nd}$ Light Squadron - Commander: Captain Brenna, later Captain May and then Lieutenant Luini. Officers: Lieutenant Pasquini, Lieutenant Corcione, Lieutenant D'Agostimi, Lieutenant Morelli, Lieutenant Venturelli, Officer Student Sergeant (IGS) Manfredini
- 3$^{rd}$ Heavy Squadron - Commander: Lieutenant Massimo Salemi (Captain since 18 July 1944). Officers: Lieutenant Pasquetti, Lieutenant Pastor, Lieutenant Pericciuoli, Lieutenant Casadei, Lieutenant Petrone
- Special Squadron (Reserve) - Commander: Lieutenant Pericciuoli; Officers - Lieutenant Venturelli, Lieutenant Brenna, Lieutenant Corcione, Lieutenant Puddinu, Lieutenant Volpi. The Special Squadron was dissolved on February 15, 1945.

## Area of employment

Back in Italy it was deployed in the area of Imperia, where he conducted anti-partisan actions between Piana Castello and Montegrande, from Caramagna to Serreta, from Castel Vecchio di Santa Maria to Nostra Signora delle Grazie. Returning to Cairo, Montenotte fought in Calizzano and on the slopes of the valley, towards Rocca delle Biscie and Bric della Mazza. Once in Cairo, he deployed his squadrons to protect the Cuneo - Mondovì-Ceva, Savona - Altare -Ceva, San Giuseppe - Acqui-Alessandria communication lines. The intense anti-partisan activity touched almost all the localities located on the Apennine ridges, Priero, Cengio, Saliceto, Montezemolo,

Noceto, Rocchetta, Mombaruzzo, Mombarcaro, Narzole, Clavesana, Mombaldone, Santo Stefano Belbo, Nizza Monferrato, Costigliole d'Alba , Canelli, Cossano, Cassinasco; in general the whole area of Val Bormida first and then of Nizzardo, with greater intensity towards the Piedmont area as tactically employed by the German Command, which considered the Exploring Group to be one of the best combat units.

# Divisional Units

### Raccolta Battalion

On December 16, 1944, the dissolved CIII "Battalion Complements" was reconstituted and took on the new name of Battalion "Collection". It was formed with personnel from the 3$^{rd}$ Artillery Regiment Command for the Command and the Allievi Battery; from the 5$^{th}$ Command Marine Infantry Regiment for the 1$^{st}$ Allievi Company; from the Command of the 6$^{th}$ Marine Infantry Regiment for the 2$^{nd}$ Allievi Company and the Marching Department. Volunteers were aggregated to this personnel, with a managerial function, who arrived following Recruitment Announcements , and the men recovered, or who will come later, from the most varied origins, including former partisans and deserters. This Battalion, despite its function of recovery and training of complements to be sent to the departments, suffered frequent and strong pressure both from part of officers of the Division is, above all, from external military and political authorities, and only the firm and decisive action of General Farina knows this lvò from the new dissolution. On January 31, 1945, the Command was taken over by Lieutenant Colonel Falconi, who, on March 12, handed it over to Lieutenant Colonel Valli. From 13 March, the "Harvest" Battalion was included in the "Valli" Tactical Group, named after its Commander and, with it, ended the hostilities on the evening of 30 April 1945 in Magenta.
First Commander of the Battalion, Major Giulio Ronchi, then Lieutenant Colonel Guido Falconi, finally Lieutenant Colonel Antonio Valli.

### Staff
At the constitution on December 16, 1944, the force amounted to:
- Command: 3 officers, 3 non-commissioned officers, 15 between graduates and troops
- 1$^{st}$ Company: 1 officers, 2 non-commissioned officers, 90 volunteers
- 2$^{nd}$ Company: 2 officers, 1 non-commissioned officers, 85 recovered
- March Department: 1 officers, 1 non-commissioned officers, 60 volunteers
- Battery: 1 officers, 1 non-commissioned officers, 40 students

As of January 1, 1945, the force amounted to 9 officers, 14 non-commissioned officers and 289 troops.
As of March 12, 1945, the force amounted to a total of 30 officers, 30 non-commissioned officers and 424 troops, divided between:
- Command - Corvette Captain: 14 officers, 8 non-commissioned officers, 90 troops
- 1$^{st}$ Company - Commander: 5 officers, 8 non-commissioned officers, 118 troopers
- 2$^{nd}$ Company - Commander: 5 officers, 8 non-commissioned officers, 117 troops
- 3$^{rd}$ Company - Commander: 6 officers, 6 non-commissioned officers, 99 troopers

### Area of employment
The Battalion was deployed between Cairo Montenotte, Forte di Altare and the Cadibona Battery. In the area he carried out the necessary training by participating, when included in the "Valli" Group, in roundups in the Val Bormida, supporting fights in Dego, Millesimo, Bragno, Roccaverana, Suole.

## "Valli" Tactical Group

On March 13, 1945, the "Valli" Tactical Group was formed, comprising the "Collezione" Battalion, the I Battalion of the 3$^{rd}$ Artillery Regiment, the 3$^{rd}$ Company of Chariot Hunters, the 5$^{th}$ Company of the 1$^{st}$ Battalion of the 6$^{th}$ Navy Infantry Regiment. The task of the "Valli" Group is to train the soldiers of the "Harvest" Battalion and to rake up and control the territory in the Val Bormida area. The "Valli" Tactical Group broke up on the evening of April 30, 1945 in Magenta.
Commander of the Group, Lieutenant Colonel Antonio Valli.

## Staff

On March 13, 1945, the date of its constitution, the strength of the Group amounted to 59 officers, 75 non-commissioned officers and 1,024 troops

## Area of employment

The Group mainly operated in the Val Bormida.

## Train Escort Department

In order to guarantee the safety of the railway trains along the Savona - San Giuseppe - Cairo - Bridges - Bistagno - Acqui - Alessandria line, a small department was set up, taken from the 3$^{rd}$ Exploring Group, which carried out the service between the stations of San Giuseppe and Acqui. Initially with a force of 15 Arditi, then the strength increased at a reduced platoon level, to then reach the maximum of consistency from October 1944 with a total of 36 men including Officers, NCOs and Troops, coming from the Scouting Group and the Health Company . On the initiative of General Farina, it was built at the I.L.V.A. of Savona, an armored tank equipped with two shielded turrets armed with heavy weapons. In the autumn the partisans blew up a bridge between Ponti and Bistagno and, when it was reactivated, the service resumed up to Strevi. From February 1945 the service was extended to Alexandria, and continued until April 25, when Allied planes destroyed the locomotive in the Acqui station. During the whole period in which he carried out the escort service, there were numerous clashes with the partisans and the air attacks suffered. The reaction of the military was always very effective and combative, always managing to repel the assaults of the partisans. First Commander of the Train Escort Department was Sergeant Poli, then Sub-Lieutenant Amedeo Rocco.

## Divisional Depot "San Marco"

The Depot of the Division was divided into two nuclei, the first located in the "Achille Papa" Barracks in Brescia and composed of actual elements of the Division and returning from convalescence or in transit, the second allocated in Lumezzane, in Val Trompia, to complete the last training period. In mid-April 1945, General Farina, with the Commander of the Depot, urged the sending of all personnel to the departments deployed on the southern front, but the SME opposed the transfer of the small Battalion, preferring to keep it available in Brescia. On the afternoon of April 25, the soldiers stationed in Brescia began to leave the barracks, the rest together with the Commander went to Lumezzane, where on the 27$^{th}$ they barricaded themselves in the school building. On the 28$^{th}$, by agreement with the CLN of Brescia, they surrendered certain of the safe conduct that guaranteed their lives. On 10 May many of them were instead taken to Sant'Eufemia della Fonte and shot, the victims were 26, including the Commander.
Commander of the Depot, Lieutenant Colonel G.N. Mario Zingarelli.

## Staff

As of April 19, 1945, 8 officers and 150 non-commissioned officers and troops were present in Brescia, while 10 officers and 240 Marò pupils were allocated in Lumezzane.

▲ Arditi of the Exploring Group of the "San Marco" Division, together with their girlfriends, have themselves portrayed in a souvenir photo shortly before boarding the translation that will take them to Germany for training at the Grafenwohr camp in March 1944 (Pisanò).

▼ Another image of the departure of the "Marcianò" Group for Germany (Pisanò).

▲ Benito Mussolini visiting the departments of the "San Marco" Division at the Grafenwohr training camp on April 24, 1944; to the left of the Duce General Princivalle, first commander of the Division (Crippa).

▼ Again Mussolini with Marshal Graziani and General Princivalle: the latter bears the frieze of a General on his helmet, provided for by the regulations of the Republican National Army (Crippa).

▲ Mussolini visited the "San Marco" Division in Germany a second time in July 1944, on the eve of the return of the departments to Italy. In the photo he talks with the new commander of the "San Marco", General Amilcare Farina (Pisanò).

▲ A wagon of the "San Marco", while leading the military of the Division to Italy in July 1944: the camouflage with the branches of the railway wagons, adopted to escape enemy aviation is interesting (Pisanò).

▲ Marò della "San Marco" intent on cleaning weapons during the return trip to Italy from training in Germany (Viziano).

▼ Marò in charge of the anti-aircraft machine gun on a convoy destined for the return of the "San Marco" to Italy at the end of the training in Germany (Viziano).

▲ The "San Marco" Division finally in Italy after the training cycle (Pisanò).

▼ Laying of a radiotelegraphic wire in a Ligurian hinterland town on the Riviera di Ponente (Pisanò).

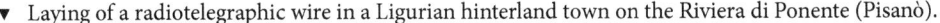

▲ A 47/32 antitank gun photographed inside a bunker manned by the marò of the "San Marco" in Liguria in September 1944 (Pisanò).

▼ 75/27 gun of the II Artillery Group Coastal post dependent on the "San Marco" (Scarone).

▲ Platoon of fusiliers of the "San Marco" Division. The photo allows you to identify all the details of the military uniforms (Crippa).

▼ The war flag of the 5th Regiment of the "San Marco" Division parades through the streets of Varazze, accompanied by Colonel Sordi, commander of the Regiment, by the Comando Company and by the 2nd Battalion (Pisanò).

▲ The deputy commander of the Harvest Battalion is decorated by a German officer (Pisanò).

▲ General Amilcare Farina, commander of the "San Marco" Division (Pisanò).

▲ Officers of the "San Marco" Division (Monterosa Archive).

▲ Soldiers of the III Connections Battalion in December 1944 (Pisanò).

▲ Soldiers of the "San Marco" on patrol in Borgio Verezzi (SV) on Christmas day 1044 (Pisanò).

▼ Shooting practice with long guns for the soldiers of the "San Marco" in the area of operations (Crippa).

▲ Drappella of the "San Marco" Division, with the winged lion and the motto "Victoria Tibi Marce", "Victory be with you, Marco: the only coat of arms of Venice with this motto is found on the Arco dei Balbi in Rovinj in Istria (Pisanò).

▼ Arditi of the Platoon Cannons of the 3rd Exploring Group tow a 7.5 cm cannon leI.G. 18 (San Marco Archive).

▲ Major Vito Marcianò, commander of the 3rd Arditi Exploring Group of the "San Marco" Division, probably photographed on the Ligurian coast in 1944 (B.A.).

▲ On the helmet of this Ardito of the Exploring Group, assigned to aiming a tow a 7.5 cm leI.G. 18, you can see the Arditi frieze, which distinguished all the soldiers of the Group. In fact, the Group originated from the II Battalion of the X Arditi Regiment "Fiamme Azzurre" (B.A.).

▲ A handful of Arditi of the Exploring Group of the "San Marco" in action during an alarm (B.A.).

▼ PAK40 anti-tank gun of the "San Marco" Division in action in Garfagnana in autumn 1944 (Pisanò).

▲ The close-up of this young volunteer of the 3rd Arditi Exploring Group allows to identify the peculiar characteristics of the uniform of this unit: the frieze of the Arditi in the Basque style, the black pentagonal insignia loaded by a skull with the dagger between a pin with the lion on the chest (BA).

▲ A department of the Exploring Group of the "San Marco" Division rests in the shade of a patch of vegetation (B.A.).

▲ Arditi of the 3rd Exploring Group on the march: the pennant reads "Marcianò", the name of the commander of the department, also known as "Gruppo Marcianò" (B.A.).

▲ Radio operator of the Infantry Division of Marina "San Marco" (Cucut).

▲ A 100/17 Howitzer of the II Hippotrained Artillery Group of the 3rd Artillery Regiment during a fire exercise on the heights of Savona (San Marco Archive).

▼ Marò squad of the Controbanda of the III Battalion of the 6th Marine Infantry Regiment in Calice Ligure in September 1944 (Scarone Archive).

▲ General Amilcare Farina during a demonstration in Altare in the winter of 1944/45 (Scarone Archive).

▲ Marò della Controbanda of the III Battalion of the 6th Regiment at the end of an operation: interesting is the use of camouflage garments, made with Italian M1929 fabric (Scarone Archive).

▼ Small collection of objects that belonged to a marin from the "San Marco": we can see the Basque badge (unfortunately damaged), the pair of gladi insignia and the chest badge for training in Germany (Waldy collection - Poland).

CORPO AUSILIARIO CC.NN.

B R I G A T A  N E R A  "A.G. A L F I E R I"
2 BATTAGLIONE
COMANDO 6 COMPAGNIA
M E D E

UFFICIO COMANDO

Mede, li 30 Novembre 1944-XXIII

AL COMANDO IV GRUPPO 3 A.R. "S. Marco"

P.D.C. **82571**

Si comunica che in data 14.9.1944 il serg. A.U. Papo' Franco ha abbattuto in Sartirana Lomellina un Caccia Bombardiere americano tipo Tander-Boold facendo fuoco con una carabina tedesca K98 a pallottola tracciante.

Non sono state prese disposizioni in merito.

Si emettono le testimonianze degli squadristi Cerutti ed il Cap. magg. Colleluori Corrado

F.to Cap.Magg. Colleluori C.
F.to Cerrutti Pietro

p- IL COMANDANTE DELLA COMPAGNIA
IL COMANDANTE IN II DELLA COMPAGNIA
F.to Ten. Consiglieri Renato

p......e......o.....
L'AIUTANTE MAGGIORE IN I.a
cap.no Mogavero Nicolò

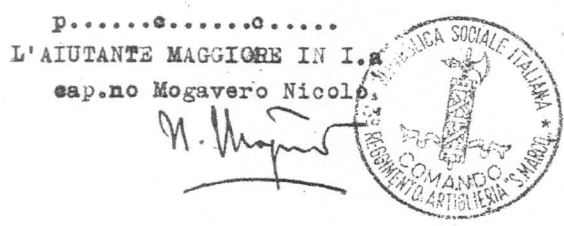

▲ Unpublished document of the Black Brigade "Alfieri" relating to the shooting down of an allied Thunderbolt aircraft, carried out by an official student of the "San Marco" Division of the IV Group of the 3rd Artillery Regiment. On 14 September 1944 the non-commissioned officer Franco Papò hit and shot down the plane in the sky of Sartirana Lomellina in the Pavia area with a German K98 carbine (Papò family archive).

▲ Military of the "San Marco" during the winter of 1944/45 (Scarone Archive).

▲ Some prisoners, captured at the end of an operation, are escorted by the marines of the "San Marco" (Pisanò).

▲ Men of the Controbanda at the end of an operation in Vara Superiore on February 27, 1945. The Bren submachine gun is a war prey (Pisanò).

▼ General Amilcare Farina, commander of the "San Marco" Division, visits the departments under his command aboard a FIAT 508 CM car.

▲ Captain Luigi Fume of the "San Marco" Infantry Division (Trovamala via Tallillo).

# 4TH "MONTEROSA" ALPINE DIVISION

Following the meetings between Mussolini and Hitler, followed by those between Graziani, Rahn and Wolf, which materialized with the subsequent Buehle - Canevari Protocol, concerning the new Army of the Italian Social Republic, the start was made for the establishment of the four new Italian Divisions, trained, armed and with similar staff to the Wehrmacht divisions, one of which is Alpina. The 4$^{th}$ "Monterosa" Alpine Division was then officially constituted on 1 January 1944 with the Centro Costituzione Grandi Unità of Vercelli with the recruits of the classes 1924 and 1925 who, in mid-February, reached, in the training camps of Heuberg, Feldstetten and Munsingen, those soldiers who, in October 1943, had formed an education battalion, to whom they had added the military ex-internees and all those Alpine departments who, having found themselves abroad on 8 September 1943, had joined the RSI and they had been sent to Munsingen. They were the "Exilles" Battalion, which came from Montenegro, the officers of the "Valle" Alpine Battalion Group, from Greece, and elements of the XX Group of Skiers from France. These were the departments that formed the backbone of the "Monterosa" Division. In the training camps he began a hard period of learning according to the techniques used in the German Army, under the constant and exhausting control of the German instructors. A totally new training also for professional soldiers or those with long years of war behind them, carried out in all weather conditions and with few rest periods. In just six months of hard work, the training and armament were completed and a good amalgamation between the Departments was achieved. On 16 July the "Monterosa" Division, fully deployed in the Munsingen camp, was reviewed by the Duce who, after a warm speech, handed the battle flags to the Regiments. Immediately after the ceremony, the transfer of the departments to Italy began, reached in the second half of July with railway trains frequently disturbed by Allied air raids, where it was deployed in Liguria, becoming part of the Liguria Army under the command of the Marshal Graziani, replacing a German division with anti-landing functions. The Division was deployed with the Command in Terrarossa di Carasco and the departments in the Riviera di Levante, located on the coast and in the hinterland, with anti-landing, control and garrison functions on the roads that connect the Ligurian coast to the Po Valley. The sector assigned to the Division, which went from Nervi to Levanto, included, was divided into two regimental subsectors: the 1$^{st}$ Alpine Regiment had that from Nervi to Sestri Levante excluded, the 2$^{nd}$ Alpine Regiment from Sestri Levante to Levanto, the 1$^{st}$ Artillery Regiment divided the Groups in support of the two Regiments. The Exploring Group and the "Ivrea" Battalion were used as divisional reserves, as well as the Pioneers Battalion, minus two Companies used by the Regiments for fortification works. The other Divisional Departments were located inland in the Cicagna area. The Departments of the "Monterosa" took possession of the pre-existing positions and built new ones, greatly improving the existing thin line of defense. It was the period in which the opening of a further front by the Allies was expected and it was not clear where the landing would take place, in any case located between Liguria and France. After the emergency in Liguria, following the Allied landing in Provence in August 1944, the "Monterosa" stopped being used as a single organic unit. Some Battalions were transferred in different periods to the front of the Western Alps, where they operated from September 1944 to April 1945, repelling the attacks of the Franco-American forces; a substantial share with the same Division Command, deployed on the occasion in Camporgiano, was transferred to the southern front, in Garfagnana, where between the Serchio river and the Apuan Alps, it blocked the way to the forces of the American 5$^{th}$ Army, participating in the offensive " Wintergewitter "of Christmas; his other Departments remained garrison in Liguria. At the end of March 1945, the Departments of the "Monterosa" Division were located as follows: in Piedmont - five Battalion, two Artillery Group and the Command of the 2nd Regiment; in Liguria - Command of the 1st Regiment, a Battalion, the Exploring Group and an Artillery Group; in Garfagnana - a Battalion, an Artillery Group and the Pioneers Battalion; in the Aosta Valley - a Battery. In the spring of 1945, when the largest nucleus of the Division was deployed in Piedmont to defend the border of the Western Alps, the Division Command took office in Samone, in the Pallavicini-Mossi castle. The end of hostilities therefore saw the "Monterosa" departments deployed on various fronts, geographically located in three distinct regions and with problems in maintaining contact with the Division Command. The "Monterosa" Division broke up on April 28, 1945, following the order to cease hostilities issued by Marshal Graziani, some of its Departments surrendered only in early May.

First Commander of the Division, Colonel Umberto Manfredini, then General Goffredo Ricci, then General Mario Carloni, finally Colonel Giorgio Milazzo.

## Organization chart

- Commander: Colonel Umberto Manfredini, then General Goffredo Ricci, then General Mario Carloni, finally Colonel Giorgio Milazzo
- Ordinance Officer: Lieutenant Vittorio Henzel
- Liaison Officer: Lieutenant Ettore Martella
- Office 1 / A Operations: Lieutenant Colonel Teodoro Anela, Captain Carlo Fonio, Lieutenant Orazio Coggi
- Office 1 / B Services: Major Aurelio Marcarino, Captain Siegel, Captain Napoleon De Kummerlin,
- Captain Ballotta, Lieutenant Braccini
- Office 1 / C Information: Captain Vincenzo Ruisi, Lieutenant Mario Cristiani, Lieutenant Rossi
- Office 1 / D Training: Captain Taggiasco, Lieutenant Pastaurenti
- Office 2 / A Staff: Major Roberto Telò, Lieutenant Bavaglioni, Lieutenant Gavazzi, Lieutenant Tolù
- Office 2 / B Personnel: Captain Luigi Ferrario
- Office 3 / A Justice: Lieutenant Colonel Cesare D'Antonio
- Court: Lieutenant Colonel Armando Farinacci, Lieutenant Colonel Policarpo Chierici, Lieutenant Beltrametti, Lieutenant Maglio
- Office 3 / B Prisoners: Second Lieutenant M. Cristiani
- Office 4 / A Intendency: Lieutenant Colonel Robertiello, Major Gaudolia, Captain Ognibene, Lieutenant Pio Ulivieri, Lieutenant Betto
- Office 4 / B Healthcare: Medical Colonel Luigi Biocca, Lieutenant Colonel Guido Fracassi
- Office 4 / C Veterinary: Captain Pausolli, Captain De Paola
- Office 4 / D Spiritual Assistance: Captain Luigi Don Miglio
- Office 5 Transport: Captain Napoleone De Kummerlin, Major Ferrari, Captain Ripandelli, Lieutenant Messerotti Welcome
- Depot: Captain R. La Manica
- Group of interpreters: Lieutenant Saitto
- Gendarmerie: Captain Simonetti, Lieutenant Peruzzi
- 1st Section GNR: Captain M. Civetta, Lieutenant Gavotti, Lieutenant Peruzzi, Lieutenant Bertucelli, Lieutenant Cerullo, Lieutenant Terrain
- UDOF: Captain Mario Caroti
- Auxiliaries: Bucci Parrasci, Augusta Murialdo
- D.K.V. n. 183: General Picker

# 1st Alpini Regiment
- Regimental Command Company
- Battaglione "Aosta":
    - 1st Company
    - 2nd Company
    - 3rd Company
    - 4th Company
    - 5th Company
- "Bassano" Battalion:
    - 6th Company
    - 7th Company
    - 8th Company
    - 9th Company
    - 10th Company
- "Intra" Battalion:
    - 11th Company
    - 12th Company
    - 13th Company
    - 14th Company
    - 15th Company
- 101st Anti - Tank Company
- Light column
- Wagons and Supply
- Transmission Company

# 2nd Alpini Regiment
- Regimental Command Company
- "Brescia" Battalion:
    - 1st Company
    - 2nd Company
    - 3rd Company
    - 4th Company
    - 5th Company
- "Morbegno" Battalion:
    - 6th Company
    - 7th Company
    - 8th Company
    - 9th Company
    - 10th Company
- "Tirano" Battalion:
    - 11th Company
    - 12th Company
    - 13th Company
    - 14th Company
    - 15th Company
- Light column
- Wagons and Supply
- Transmission Company

**1st Mountain Artillery Regiment**
- Regimental Command Battery
- 1st "Aosta" Donned Artillery Group:
  - Command Battery
  - 1st Battery
  - 2nd Battery
  - 3rd Battery 75/13 howitzers
- 2nd "Bergamo" Donned Artillery Group:
  - Command Battery
  - 4th Battery
  - 5th Battery
  - 6th Battery 75/13 howitzers
- 3rd Submitted Artillery Group "Verona" (later "Vicenza"):
  - Command Battery
  - 7th Battery
  - 8th Battery
  - 9th Battery 75/13 howitzers
- 4th "Mantua" Hippotrained Artillery Group:
  - Command Battery
  - 10th Battery
  - 11 Battery
  - 12th Battery 100/17 howitzers (later FH18-10.5)
- Light column
- Anti-tank battery

**1st Exploring Group (Bersaglieri)**
- Command Department
- 1st Light Squadron
- 2nd Light Squadron

3rd Heavy Squadron, equipped with Pak 40 anti-tank guns and 75/10 IG 18 howitzers.
The Exploring Group, after the death of the major commander Cadelo, took his name.

**Divisional Units**
- Pioneer Battalion:
  - Command Company
  - 1st Company
  - 2nd Company
  - 3rd Company
- Transmission Battalion:
  - Command Company
  - 1st Company
  - 2nd Company
  - 3rd Company
- Transportation Battalion:
  - Command Company
  - 1st Chart Company
  - 2nd Hippotrained Company
  - 3rd Hippotrained Company

- 1st Truck Company
           - 2nd Truck Company
   - Health Department:
       - 1st Healthcare Company
       - 101st Healthcare Company
       - 2 Hospital Units
       - Surgical Nucleus
       - Ambulance section
   - Intendency Department on 6 Companies:
       - Administration
       - Bakers
       - Butchers
       - Veterinary
       - Workshop
       - Subsistence
- Divisional Anti-Tank Company
- Complements Battalion "Ivrea"
- Education Battalion formed in October 1943 and disbanded in January 1944.
- Field Gendarmerie Department and three Military Police Sections provided by the G.N.R.
- Military Court and Prison
- Divisional Deposit

On February 2, 1945, the "Cadore" Alpine Battalion, coming from the "Raggruppamento Cacciatori degli Appennini", was incorporated into the "Monterosa" Division as an exploration unit. During the stay in Liguria, 6 alarm companies were set up, taken from the Battalion, and grouped into the "Saluzzo" and "Vestone" Operational Battalions outside the framework, which carried out security tasks in the rear, with little commitment due to the lack of cohesion of these picking departments.

## Total Staff

The overall strength of the Division amounted to about 19,500 men including Officers, NCOs, Graduates and Troops. The Divisional Departments had a total strength of about 5,500 men, the Regimental Departments of 550. Each Battalion was formed by: Company Command, three Company of riflemen, one of heavy weapons. Each Company was made up of 220 men, the Heavy of 300, for an overall strength of the Battalion of about 1,100 / 1,200 men. The strength of the Departments of the Artillery Regiment was about 450 men, the Groups were about 1,100 men and the Batteries of 300/350.

## Weaponses

- 480 M.G.42 machine guns, Breda 37 machine guns were present in some departments
- 46 Mortars 80 mm
- 37 Howitzers 75/13 Skoda
- 12 Howitzers 100/17, replaced by German 10.5 FH 18 howitzers
- 33 anti-tank and infantry guns, Pak 40s and German 75/10 IG 18 howitzers.
- 15 Machine guns 20 mm
- wide range of Panzerfaust

The 20 75/43 anti-tank guns were replaced by 36 Panzerschrecks.

## Vehicles

The Exploring Group returned from Germany with these means: 20 Trucks, 6 Cars, 12 Motorcycles, 1 Ambulance, complete set of bicycles. The rest of the Departments had a shortage that was close to half of the quadrupeds foreseen by the armament tables and a third of the means of transport. As of March 1, 1945, according to the report on the situation of the Italian units drawn up by the German Command, the "Monterosa" was equipped with: 96 motorcycles, 89 cars, 127 trucks, 14 tractors, 678 carts, 618 bicycles, 2198 horses and mules. Of these means, a considerable amount was not available because it was out of use.

## Losses of the "Monterosa" Division

Throughout 2004, 1,097 fallen have been identified, of which 38 unknown and 342 killed by the partisans, of which 133 after 25 April.

# 1st Alpini Regiment

The 1st Alpine Regiment was established in Aosta on December 24, 1943, including the "Aosta", "Bassano" and "Intra" Alpine Battalions, the Chariot Hunters Company (16th), the Connections Company and other regimental departments. . In 1945 it incorporated the 17th Autonomous Company of Captain Scattolin. Transferred to Germany in the early months of 1945, he was trained in the camps of Heuberg, Feldstetten and Munsingen, where he received the battle flag from the Duce on 16 July 1944. The return to Italy immediately began where, between the end of July and the beginning of August, it was deployed, as an anti-landing function, in Liguria on the Riviera di Levante, with the Command stationed in Cicagna and the Battalion deployed to defend the sector between Nervi and Lavagna, also providing for the safety of communication and supply routes in the hinterland threatened by the action of the partisans. Following the landing of the Allies in Provence, the Regiment received the order to transfer the "Bassano" Battalion to Piedmont on the front of the Western Alps, between Val Varaita and Val Maira, in the province of Cuneo. At the end of October, the 1st Regiment began the transfer to the Garfagnana front. The Regimental Command moved with the "Intra" Battalion, the 1st Company of the "Aosta" Battalion and the regimental departments. The headquarters of the Command was located in Castelnuovo Garfagnana, while the Departments, dependent on it, lined up from Monte Altissimo to Monte Romecchio, in the Serchio Valley. The Regiment remained in Garfagnana until February 1945, actively participating in all the clashes that developed in the winter of 1944/45, including the "Wintergewitter" Christmas offensive. At the end of February '45, having left the "Intra" Battalion in the Garfagnana, the 1st Regiment returned to Liguria, located between Carasco and San Colombano, with the dependent departments located between Sestri Levante, Terrarossa and Borgonovo, where it remained until the end of hostilities , under the command of a Combat Group including the Regimental units, the "Cadelo" Exploring Group, the "Birds" Battalion of the "San Marco" Division, and all the other "Monterosa" units remaining in Liguria. On 24 April 1945, all the dependent Departments grouped together, the withdrawal towards the Po Valley and the Po began, to be reached through the Scoffera Pass. On days 25, 26 and 27 it fought against the Allied avant-gardes on the Entella, at the Ruta Pass and in Recco. On the 27th afternoon, in Uscio, the entire force under the command of Colonel Pasquali, surrounded by the Allied troops, noting the uselessness of the continuation of the fighting, negotiated the surrender receiving the honor of arms from the Americans.

First Commander of the Regiment, Lieutenant Colonel Armando Farinacci, subsequently, until the end of hostilities, Colonel Aldo Pasquali.

## Regimental Departments

They include the Regimental Command Company, the Light Column (transport), the Connections Company, the 101st Tank Hunters Company, a Cannon Platoon. These departments were located at the headquarters of the Regimental Command both in Liguria and in Garfagnana. It was on this front that the Chariot Hunters Company and the Regimental Command Company were most involved. In particular, they distinguished themselves in the defense of Quota 832, a key position that barred access to the Americans, maintaining possession until February 1945 when they left the front. Back in Liguria they were stationed between Carasco and San Colombano, sharing the fate of the Regiment until the end of hostilities.

## "Aosta" Battalion

Returning at the end of July from training in Germany, the "Aosta" Battalion was deployed in Liguria in the Riviera di Levante, with the Command in Recco and the Companies deployed in anti-landing function from Nervi to Camogli. Its Departments, in competition with others of the Division, were also employed in the task of controlling the rolling stock, which connect the coast with the Po Valley, and in contrasting the partisan formations. At the end of September, when the "Bassano" Battalion was transferred to Piedmont, it expanded its area of operations up to the town of Rapallo, making the task of controlling the area even more demanding, given the greater defense sector assigned and the reduced forces. available dispersed over multiple garrisons. These tasks were carried out until the transfer of the Battalion to Piedmont. In October the 1$^{st}$ Company of the Battalion was sent to the Garfagnana front, joined to the "Brescia" Battalion, on the front line in the Serchio Valley. Once the transfer was completed, and as soon as it entered the line without the possibility of getting acquainted with the terrain and carrying out the necessary reconnaissance, on the day of October 28 it had to endure a very hard fight against the Brazilian troops, who attacked the positions, defended by the three platoons of the Company, with a force of three Battalions. The attack was successful and some cornerstones were lost, but on the 30$^{th}$ the counterattack was carried out which regained the lost positions and restored the front to the previous situation. The survivors of the 1$^{st}$ Company also participated in the counterattack. The total losses of the Company totaled about 80 men including dead, wounded and prisoners. The 1$^{st}$ Company remained in Garfagnana until February 1945, when it returned to Liguria and reunited with the rest of the Battalion. In March 1945, the "Aosta" Battalion was transferred to Piedmont, on the front of the Western Alps, deploying its Companies to defend the Stura Valley, with the Command at the Terme di Vinadio and its Companies deployed between Mount Ténibres and the Collalunga. On April 23, the order came to prepare for the retreat towards the plain. The Battalion reunited its companies, on 27 April agreed to surrender with the partisans and broke up in Dronero. The 3$^{rd}$ Company refused the surrender agreement and headed for Cuneo where it joined the other troops retreating towards Turin, arrived in the free zone of Strambino Romano continued towards Ivrea, where it surrendered to the Americans on May 5, 1945.
First Commander of the Battalion, Captain Appoggi, subsequently Major Paolo M. Guarini.

## "Bassano" Battalion

The "Bassano" Battalion was reconstituted in Bassano del Grappa on 24 December 1943 and placed in the 1$^{st}$ Alpine Regiment of the "Monterosa" Division being formed. Transferred to Germany at the beginning of '44, he was assigned to the Heuberg and Feldstetten camps to carry out training and complete the staff and equipment. Taking the oath on July 16, he returned to Italy at the end of July 1944, to be deployed in Liguria, with an anti-landing function, in the sector of the Riviera di Levante, with the Companies located between Camogli and Rapallo, with Departments in Portofino and Rezzoaglio. Following the landing of the Allies in Provence, which threatened to circumvent the Po Valley, on September 15, the "Bassano" began the transfer to Piedmont, in the Province of Cuneo, making the journey by truck along the Genoa-Alessandria-Asti route. Moncalieri-Saluzzo. From Saluzzo the Battalion went up to Casteldelfino, in Val Varaita, where it placed the Command, with three Companies, while in Acceglio, in Val Maira, it deployed the other two. At the end of September the deployment of the Companies was completed, having taken possession of all the surrounding hills and passes. Some hills had previously been occupied by French maquis and partisans, but already on 25 September the "Bassano" had taken possession of them again, improving the fortification works, thus giving consistency to the defense of the sector, preparing fire plans, positions for weapons, organizing supplies, also preparing for the winter accommodation, particularly delicate considering the difficulties in living at a high altitude with minimum temperatures of 15/20 ° below zero. The manned hills were located at altitudes between 2500 and 2880 meters above sea level, between Monviso and La Maddalena, with the Colle dell'Agnello, St. Véran, Longet, Autaret, Maurin. The activities on the border line in the winter period were limited to patrol activities, due to the particularly harsh climatic conditions with abundant snowfall, frequent avalanches and frost, which caused considerable difficulties in supplying the garrisons. At the end of winter, these activities became more intensive, with actions carried out across the border, in the Val Tinea in St. Véran and Fontgillard, in the Ubaye Valley up to St. Paul. For their part, the French attacked the Colle dell'Agnello and St. Véran, with forces consisting of at least two companies, but were repulsed by the Alpini of the "Bassano". If the activity on the border line was reduced, this cannot be said for the contrast to the partisan forces, particularly active in the Varaita, Maira and Stura valleys. Departments of the "Bassano" were also employed in large anti-partisan round-up operations, in collaboration with other Italian and German departments, while, for the defense of their supply lines, a special mobile counter-band was set up, under the command of Lieutenant Adami, which had notable successes. On April 25, 1945 the "Bassano" Command received the order to fall back towards the plain, on the 26 the Commander, authorized by the officers to ask the partisans not to interfere with the departure of the Battalion to avoid the shedding of further blood from both parties, instead negotiated the surrender, agreeing, for the Alpini, the freedom to go home with a pass, while the officers and non-commissioned officers had to remain in place to be handed over to the Americans. As soon as they laid down their arms the pacts were not respected, Alpini isolated or in small groups were stopped and killed by partisans who did not recognize the pass, while the officers and non-commissioned officers were locked up in the "Musso" barracks in Saluzzo. For several days many of them were subjected to torture, violence and finally killed, until on 7 May the Americans took over the survivors to transport them to prison camps. The partisans unleashed their violence in particular against the components of the counter-band, many of whom were passed to arms. First Commander of the Battalion, Lieutenant Colonel Cipriano Nanni, subsequently Major Giuseppe Alberton, then Major Mario Molinari.

**"Intra" Battalion**
The "Intra" Battalion was reconstituted in Aosta on February 15, 1944, framed in the $1^{st}$ Alpine Regiment, and transferred to Germany to train in the Munsingen camp. Returning to Italy at the end of July 1944, he was deployed in Liguria, in the Riviera di Levante, as an anti-landing function to defend the sector between the Rezzoaglio-mare and Passo del Bocco-Lavagna lines, with the Battalion Command located in Zoagli. At the end of October the "Intra" Battalion began the transfer to the Garfagnana front where, from 28 October, it entered the Serchio Valley in line. It took over the sector that went from Monte Altissimo to Monte Grottorotondo, passing through Monte Corchia, Pania della Croce and Pania Secca, a line for Alpini, due to the altitude and harshness of the mountain, consisting of high peaks and very sour. On Monte Altissimo it connected with the $148^{th}$ German Division, which guarded the western side of the Apuan Alps up to the coast. Given the length of the defensive line, only the points where it could be easier for the enemy to enter were manned. The Command of the Battalion was placed near the Freddone bridge, the $11^{th}$ Company between the Most High and the Corchia; the $12^{th}$ Company between the Pania della Croce and the Pania Secca; the $13^{th}$ Company on the western side of the Altissimo, the $14^{th}$ Company at the Foce di Mosceta between the Corchia and the Pania della Croce, while a detachment remained in Isola Santa with the task of protecting the supply lines. Opposite the Brazilians of the F.E.B., replaced in early November by the Americans of the $92^{nd}$ "Buffalo" Division, made up of black men. Unfortunately, even in Garfagnana there were substantial nuclei of partisans who not only made the supply lines and connections dangerous, but actively collaborated with the Allies, both during some attacks

launched in November by the Americans, and by providing information on the locations of the Departments. deployed in defense of the front line. On November 4, the first attack was launched against the defensive line of the Battalion and the suture with the marines of the II Battalion-6th "San Marco" Regiment, which, after an initial success, was rejected by the counterattack launched by the Italian Departments and Germans. The attacks were repeated in mid-November, and continued with less intensity until the beginning of December, in a succession of attacks and counterattacks where the Alpini always demonstrated their combativeness. The "Intra" Battalion participated in the "Wintergewitter" Christmas offensive, with solid patrols to keep the units in front of it busy, therefore, once the offensive was over, it went to occupy the new defensive line, moved further south on a line that from Pania Secca it went to Calomini, which had a greater defensive depth and better tactical positions, while the old line became the second defensive line and the defense gained breath. The "Intra" remained deployed on its new positions until mid-April 1945, when, following the breakthrough of the Gothic Line in the Adriatic sector as a result of the final offensive by the Allies, it began to withdraw towards the Po Valley, supporting rearguard against the Americans and the partisans. On the night of April 18, the units of the Battalion began the retreat. On the 19th the "Intra" arrived in Casola, continuing on the 21st for the Cerreto pass with the task of guarding it and ensuring the transit of other departments. The pass, however, was already occupied by American troops and the Battalion then returned to Fivizzano, from where it continued towards Licciana Nardi-Bagnone, being attacked by partisans and deserters of a Bersaglieri Battalion of the "Italy" Division. The surprise was great and the losses high. After the ambush, the Battalion climbed over the Cisa and descended towards Parma, reaching Fornovo, where, on the orders of Gen Carloni, it formed a combat group with the "Bergamo" Artillery Group. On April 29, 1945, in Fornovo Taro, the "Intra" Battalion closed its operational life by surrendering to the Brazilian troops with the honor of arms. First Commander of the Battalion, Lieutenant Colonel Francesco Giorda, then Major Aurelio Marcarino, then Captain Mario Fornasari, finally Captain Franco Appoggi.

## 2nd Alpini Regiment

The 2nd Alpine Regiment was established in Milan on 1 January 1944, including the "Brescia", "Morbegno" and "Tirano" Battalions, the Regimental Command Company, the Connections Company, the 102nd Tank Hunters Company, the Light Column ( Salmerie), a Cannon Platoon. He trained in the Heuberg and Munsingen camps, where on July 16, 1944 he received the fighting flag. Returning to Italy at the end of July, he was deployed in Liguria, in the Riviera di Levante, with the departments located in the left divisional defensive sector, between Sestri Levante and Levanto, as an anti-landing function on the coast and, towards the hinterland along the passes and Apennine ridges, to defend the communication routes with the Po Valley from partisans' incursions. Having landed in Provence in mid-August, the Regiment transferred the "Tirano" Battalion to the Alpine front in early September to defend the Montgenèvre pass and the Val Chisone passes. At the end of October he transferred the "Brescia" Battalion to the Garfagnana front (to which the 1st Compagnia dell'Aosta was aggregated) where he remained until mid-February 1945, when he rejoined the Regiment. The Regimental Command, with the Regimental Departments, and the "Morbegno" Battalion, operated for the logistical security of the rear, participating in the large anti-partisan round-up operations of the September-October period. In early February 1945 the Regimental Command, with its Regimental Departments, and the "Morbegno" Battalion, were transferred to the western Alps front, taking sides in defense of the Valleys of Viù, Ala and Val Grande, with the Command in Lanzo. In March he was joined by the "Brescia" Battalion which deployed in the Locana Valley to the right of the "Morbegno". With the arrival of the "Brescia", the Regiment extended over a front of about one hundred kilometers, between the Valle di Locana and the Val Chisone, on a defensive line where German units were also located, at an altitude always higher than 2,000 meters with positions and observers between 2,500 and 3,000 meters, with high mountain ranges that made the valleys incommunicable. Until the end of the hostilities, only a garrison and anti-partisan activity was carried out. On 25 April the order to retreat to the Command of the 2nd Regiment arrived, the order was sent to the "Morbegno": withdraw the garrisons at the border, gather the Companies and go down to Lanzo. While the departments of the "Morbegno" began the preparations for the retreat, the Compagnia Cacciatori di Carri left for the plain abandoning the Regiment and the Light Column passed with the partisans. The Commander, two officers and a few men remained at the Regimental Command, who were forced to ask the partisans to surrender, it was the morning of April 26, 1945. Also in this case the agreement reached was not respected, so that five were shot officers, five non-commissioned officers and three Alpini.

First Commander of the Regiment, Colonel Umberto Manfredini, then Colonel Policarpo Chierici, then Colonel Giorgio Milazzo, finally Captain Lorenzo Malingher, shot on May 5 by the partisans.

## Regimental Departments

They include the Regimental Command Company and the Light Column (transport), set up in Milan on January 1, 1944, the 102nd Tank Hunters Company set up on February 26 in Verona and the Connections Company. These departments operated, both in Liguria and in Piedmont, always reporting directly to the Command of the 2nd Regiment, participating, in collaboration with other departments, also in sweeping operations in the Ligurian hinterland. In the night between 25 and 26 April 1945, without even taking into consideration a hypothesis of surrender to the partisans, aliquots of the Regimental Command Company and the Tank Hunters Company abandoned the headquarters of the Command of the 2nd Regiment, heading, in arms and completely truck, towards Turin and the plain, surrendering on April 26 at Tronzano Vercellese. The next day the Company was sent to Biella where it broke up. The C.L.N. from Biella had proposed to them to join the partisan formations to go and defend Trieste from the Titoites, but since the idea was immediately abandoned, the Alpini and officers received a pass and were set free. The Light Column instead passed almost entirely with the partisans and some of them will be used to guard the former fellow soldiers prisoners in the Collegio di Lanzo.

**"Brescia" Battalion**

The "Brescia" Battalion, heir to the traditions of the "Vestone" Battalion of the "Tridentina" Division, was constituted in Brescia on January 1, 1944, and included in the staff of the 2nd Alpine Regiment. Transferred to Germany, he completed his training in the Munsingen camp, returning to Italy at the end of July 1944. He was deployed in Liguria, with the role of strategic reserve of the Regiment, with the Companies deployed in the hinterland in the area north of the Bracco Pass and the Command placed in San Pietro Vara. This line-up was maintained from the end of July to October 1944, when it was transferred to the Garfagnana front. During its stay in the Ligurian hinterland, the Battalion was employed in anti-partisan round-up operations, detaching the 2nd Company in Varzi, a garrison that was attacked by two partisan brigades in mid-September and forced to surrender, with the loss of more than half of the personnel. The transfer began on October 25th and on October 28th the "Brescia" entered the line, replacing the German departments of the 42nd Jaeger, siding astride the Serchio river, placing the Command in Palleroso, the companies on the river bed to the west as far as Campo and the 1st Compagnia dell'"Aosta", attached to it, on the left bank towards Treppignana. The Battalion, thus deployed, constituted the left wing of the "Monterosa" deployment in front of the US 5th Army. As soon as he arrived on the line, the Brazilian troops immediately tried to verify the combativeness of the new arrivals, unleashing a series of attacks on 28 and 29 October, against the Compagnia dell'"Aosta", which, due to the preponderance of the attacking forces and the perfect knowledge of the ground, they were successful. The Commander of the "Brescia", who rushed immediately with the reinforcements, helped to block the infiltration of the Brazilian units, allowing the Italo-German reinforcements to prepare a new defensive line. At dawn on the 30th the counterattack was carried out on two directions, in the area of the salient created following the

Brazilian offensive the "Brescia" which, in the evening, had regained the positions lost on the 28$^{th}$. The front on the initial defensive line was restored. , there were no actions of particular importance until Christmas, except for the daily patrol activity, the mortar fire and the continuous cannonade work by the Americans. During the "Wintergewitter" offensive, the "Brescia" participated with a company, attached to the Germans of the 285$^{th}$ Regiment, in the attack on Barga and, with the remaining companies, in the attack on Gallicano to the right of the Serchio. The offensive was successful and, in addition to the capture of a large quantity of weapons, ammunition, food and other kinds of comfort, it led to an improvement of the first defensive line, while the old positions were equipped with a second defensive line, allowing a significant improvement. the depth of the defensive sector. The "Brescia" remained on its new positions until February 1945, when it was replaced by the Bersaglieri of the 1$^{st}$ Battalion of the 1$^{st}$ Regiment of the "Italy" Division, starting the transfer to Liguria starting from 13 February. After a period of rest in La Spezia, he reached Genoa on foot and on 7 March he was reviewed by Marshal Graziani. He then went on to Piedmont directed to Turin in translation. In the night between 12 and 13, between Villafranca and Villanova d'Asti, the translation suffered a bomb attack, the partisans had placed a mine under the rails which exploded when the convoy passed. 17 Alpini died and about thirty were injured. From mid-March, the "Brescia" completed the transfer to the Canavese, siding in the Locana Valley, and dell'Orco, to Pont Canavese, with the Companies located at the Galisia Pass, Ceresole Reale and Locana, with border defense tasks of the Alps by French infiltrations. The Battalion returned after four months under the command of the 2$^{nd}$ Regiment. The "Brescia" at the end of April, unable to maintain contact with the Regimental Command, gave a mandate to its companies to negotiate the conditional surrender with the local partisans: prisoner officers and Alpini at liberty. Each Company dissolved in the localities where they were located, the pacts were respected and there was no violence. First Commander of the Battalion, Major Aldo Pasquali, subsequently, Captain Locatelli, finally Captain Felice Ferrarese.

**"Morbegno" Battalion**

The "Morbegno" Battalion was formed in Morbegno at the end of 1943 and incorporated into the 2$^{nd}$ Regiment on January 1, 1944. Transferred to Germany, it completed training in the fields of Heuberg and Munsingen, returning to Italy at the end of July 1944, to be deployed in Liguria, in the Riviera di Levante, in defense of the sector between Moneglia and Levanto, carrying out anti-landing defense functions. Following the transfer of the "Tirano" to Piedmont, the "Morbegno" expanded the defensive sector up to Sestri Levante. He was employed in the operations, arranged by the Division and by the Board of Directors. "Lombardia", for the safety of the divisional rear lines and for the control of the roads that, crossing the Apennine passes, connect Liguria with the Po Valley. During the winter period, small garrisons were left on the coast, apart from Levanto where the entire 6$^{th}$ Company remained, while the bulk of the Departments were deployed inland to guard the road junctions and the Bracco pass, manned by the 8$^{th}$ Company. Numerous attacks and ambushes against the Alpini of "Morbegno", the 8$^{th}$ Company alone suffered 8 in three months. At the beginning of February 1945, the order for the transfer to Piedmont, on the front of the Western Alps, arrived at the "Morbegno". Gathered in Sestri Levante, he reached Genoa on foot and by truck, from where he continued by train to Asti, to leave again for the Lanzo Valleys (TO) between 6 and 7 February. Arriving in the Lanzo Valleys, he deployed his Companies between the two valleys that branch off from Lanzo: the Val d'Ala, from which the Val Grande branches off, and the Val di Viù, replacing the German and parà departments of the "Folgore" Regiment. The "Morbegno" deployed the Command in Ceres and deployed the Companies at the head of the valleys with posts advanced on the line of passes: the 8$^{th}$ Company in Usseglio, the 7$^{th}$ Company in Balme, the 6$^{th}$ Company in Forno Alpi Graie, the 10$^{th}$ Company in Ceres , the 9$^{th}$ Company in Viù. The 8$^{th}$ Company detached a Platoon to Malciausia and a detachment to Lago della Rossa, places where there are hydroelectric basins of strategic importance; the 7$^{th}$ Company a Platoon on the border with France at the Gastaldi Refuge. This line-up was maintained until the night of April 26, 1945. During this period, no offensive actions were carried out by the French troops, apart from a single attempt to encroach on the Lago della Rossa immediately rejected with losses on both sides. Major problems came from the actions of the partisans, not so much at the head of the valleys, as in the villages downstream from the headquarters of the "Morbegno" Command, such as Mezzenile, Pessinetto, Traves and Chiaves, headquarters of important groups of partisans, creating problems for the logistic lines. This was obviated with continuous raking actions carried out in collaboration with the Regimental Command Company stationed in Lanzo. Among the most important actions, that of 11 April towards Pian Audi and Corio, even if without significant results. On the evening of April 25, 1945, the order arrived at the "Morbegno" from the Command of the 2nd Regiment, to withdraw the border guards, group the 6th, 7th, 10th Companies in Ceres and get off at Lanzo, while the 8th and 9[a] had to go down directly on Lanzo. Since it was necessary to wait for the seconded garrisons and the distances from Lanzo oscillated between thirty and thirty-five kilometers, it would have been necessary that the garrison had remained stable in Lanzo, given that at least until the 26th afternoon the folding of the "Morbegno" could not be completed. Instead, Lanzo's garrison fell apart, accepting surrender on the 26th, and communications were interrupted with the Companies and the Battalion Command. Thus it was that, having reached the headquarters of the individual companies, no longer receiving orders from the higher command, the individual commanders were approached by emissaries of the partisans who offered to surrender. Totally devoid of connection, there was no other choice but to accept surrender under the conditions imposed: Alpini at liberty with a safe conduct, officers prisoners. The "Morbegno" broke up on April 26th. The pacts were not respected and many officers, non-commissioned officers and Alpini were captured by other partisan formations, concentrated in the Episcopal College of Lanzo Torinese and in the Germagnano paper mill, from where many officers, non-commissioned officers and Alpini were transferred to the places where they had fought and shot. on site. Many others were subjected to violence and beatings, until May 5, when an American column arrived and took over the surviving prisoners.

First Commander of the Battalion, Major Luigi Pagliano, then Captain Adriano Roggero, then Captain Lorenzo Malingher, finally Captain Carlo Pezzolini.

**"Tirano" Battalion**

The "Tirano" Battalion was established in Tirano in 1943, incorporated into the 2nd Regiment on 1 January 1944, and transferred to Germany, in the fields of Heuberg and Munsingen, to carry out training. He began his return to Italy on 19 July 1944, starting from Munsingen, reaching the Ligurian coast of the Riviera di Levante on the 26. He was deployed to defend the coastal sector from Sestri Levante to Moneglia with anti-landing defense tasks, taking possession of the positions sold by the Germans which he provided to improve. The positions of the "Tirano" were, as early as July 29, immediately targeted by the Allied air force which, on very precise indications from the partisans, hit the targets with precision, causing the first casualties. The raids were thwarted by the anti-aircraft which, one morning, managed to shoot down three planes. The fallen of the "Tirano" were the first of the "Monterosa". After the air raids, the "Tirano" was not particularly busy, given the quiet activity of garrison of the coast and the non-participation in the roundups in the hinterland. After the Allied landing in Provence on August 15, the Battalion was ordered to prepare for the transfer to Piedmont, on the front of the Western Alps in the Montgenèvre sector. On 9 September the "Tirano" departed from Liguria, arriving in Cesana (TO) on 11. On the 13th he entered the line giving the change to German units of the 85th Regiment of the 5th Alpine Division "Gams", inserting himself between the lines of the 85th Regiment on which he tactically depended. It was deployed on a sector that ran at altitudes above 2,000 meters above sea level, from Claviere passing through Rocca Clary and Punta Rascià up to Mount Gimont, with the last fighting post at Mount Chenaillet at 2,650 meters. The Battalion Command was placed in line at Punta Pascià, while the rear base remained in Pinerolo, the advanced base was formed in Cesana and Bousson became the headquarters of the

Company which in turn descended from the front line for the rest shift. The sector taken in charge was well fortified, with bunkers, tunnels, barracks and barracks that had been prepared for some time and equipped with stoves and cots to fight the intense cold and heavy snowfall. Opposite, in equally fortified positions, metropolitan and colonial Americans and French were lined up. The action of French artillery and mortars was constant, which was met with parsimony due to the shortage of ammunition. As for the activities of the partisans, however, the situation on the line was calm, the population feared to see the French descend and knew their arrogance. There were some problems instead towards the back base of Pinerolo, where the anti-French sentiment was less strong and the presence of the partisan bands present in the Val Chisone was stronger. Particularly delicate were the journeys of the commanders between Cesana, Claviere and the front line, on roads and mule tracks that ran for long stretches under the full control of enemy observers, who promptly called in the artillery. In mid-October the French, with a surprise action, occupied the outpost of Chenaillet, promptly reoccupied with a joint action of the Alpini of the "Tirano" and the Germans who, on the 21$^{st}$, with a pincer action, overcame the French defenders , a colonial ward. In the action, Renato Assante, an Italian born in Turkey who had retained his Italian citizenship and had come to Italy to enlist as a volunteer, fell at the head of the attacking forces, joining the RSI Army after 8 September, to whose memory the MOVM, the only one of the Division, will be granted. New action on 23 December, when a patrol of Alpine skiers, from the "Tirano" and Germans, made a foray into the opposing lines by blowing up the fortifications of M. Janus, from where the French patrols departed. So until spring the activity was carried out only with patrols and counter patrols, due to the abundant snowfalls that prevented other actions. On 23 April 1945 the order came to the "Tirano" Command to begin the retreat towards the plain but, due to a sudden attack by the French in the direction of Claviere, promptly rejected, only on the 26$^{th}$ the Battalion was able to reunite in Cesana from where, in columns with the departments of the "Gams", he reached Pinerolo and then Rivoli Torinese. During the march, the Cannon Platoon abandoned the Battalion surrendering itself to the partisans, while the Commander, the adjutant major and the Chaplain surrendered to the partisans as hostages to ensure a bloodless retreat for their men. Once in Rivoli, the C.L.N. he proposed surrender to the "Tirano", with the same conditions offered by other partisan formations: freedom for the Alpini and delivery of the officers to the Allies, this proposal was accepted and the "Tirano" broke up. Also on this occasion the agreements made with the local partisans were not respected and many soldiers were captured and taken to the New Prisons of Turin, where they suffered violence, torture and shootings. Only on May 8, the Americans took over the surviving prisoners to take them to prison camps. The 12$^{th}$ Company did not accept the surrender and, with elements of the other Companies that had joined, continued towards Turin where, having learned of the message of Marshal Graziani, it negotiated the surrender with the partisans of the "Val Sangone" brigade and broke up. In this case the pacts were respected and the officers were handed over to the Americans without violence of any kind. First Commander of the Battalion, Major Augusto Gardini, then Lieutenant Colonel Mario Polo, then Major Serafino Glarey.

## 1$^{st}$ Alpine Artillery Regimento

The 1$^{st}$ Alpine Artillery Regiment was established in Pavia on January 1, 1944, including in its staff, in addition to the Regimental Command Battery, the "Aosta", "Bergamo", "Verona" (later "Vicenza") each of three groups. Battery of 75/13 and the Hippotrained group "Mantova" on three Battery of 100/17. Transferred to Germany, he completed training in the fields of Feldstetten, Heuberg, Gruorn and Gaensewag. On July 16 he received the combat flag and began the operations for the transfer to Italy. Returned to Italy at the end of July, he was deployed in Liguria in support of the anti-landing line from Nervi to Levanto, with the "Bergamo" Group in support of the 1$^{st}$ Alpine Regiment, the "Aosta" Group in support of the 2$^{nd}$ Alpine Regiment , the "Vicenza" Group in the Leivi area and the "Mantova" Group in the Caperana area, the Regimental Command was placed first in Cicagna then in San Colombano. From 27 July to 2 November, it also incorporated the

6th Artillery Group P.C. deployed in the Chiavari area. Following the Allied landing in Provence, the Regiment lost the "Vicenza" Group, sent to Piedmont, on the Western Alps front, to defend the Alpine passes. At the end of October the Command, the Regimental Command Battery, the "Bergamo" and "Mantova" Groups were transferred to the Garfagnana front, operating in support of the Italo-German units deployed in the sector of the Apuan Alps, with the Command stationed in Poggio and the Group "Bergamo" and "Mantova" lined up to the left of the defensive sector. During the operational cycle in the Garfagnana, three German artillery groups present in the area were also employed by the Regiment and, in the "Wintergewitter" offensive, all the German-Italian artillery deployed for the action was directed by Colonel Grossi. In February 1945, the Regimental Command, the Regimental Command Battery and the "Mantova" Group returned to Liguria and then continued towards Piedmont, the new location of the 1st Artillery Regiment. The "Bergamo" Group remained until the end of hostilities on the Garfagnana front, forming a Combat Group with the "Intra" Battalion at the end of April. The "Aosta" Group, on the other hand, was always employed in Liguria, participating in the cleaning operations of the communication routes towards the Po Valley. The Regimental Command disbanded in Ivrea at the end of April 1945, following the order to lay down arms given by Marshal Graziani.

First Commander of the Regiment, Lieutenant Colonel Binda, then Lieutenant Colonel Cesare D'Antonio, then Lieutenant Colonel (later Colonel) Luigi Grossi.

## Regimental Command Battery

It was established in Pavia on 1 January 1944, framed in the 1st Alpine Artillery Regiment, and transferred to Germany to train in the Heuberg and Gaensewag camps. She returned to Italy she was in the retinue of the Regimental Command following its history and final fate.

### 1st Artillery Group "Aosta"

The "Aosta" donned Artillery Group, armed with 12 Skoda 75/13 World War I howitzers, already in service in the Royal Army Groups, was established in Pavia on January 1, 1944, incorporated into the 1st Alpine Artillery Regiment, and moved to Germany to train in Heuberg and Gruorn camps. He returned to Italy at the end of July and took up a position in Liguria in support of the 2nd Alpine Regiment in the defensive sector between Sestri Levante and Levanto, with the Command stationed in Velva. In cooperation with the other Divisional Departments remaining in Liguria, he participated in the anti-partisan roundup operations aimed at keeping the communication routes of the rear areas that lead to the Po Valley free. On the night of April 24, the "Aosta" Group gathered its Departments and rejoined in Chiavari with the remaining Departments of the "Monterosa". The column, under the command of Colonel Pasquali, Commander of the 1st Alpine Regiment, moved westward at dawn on April 25th. It was immediately attacked by the avant-garde of two American regiments equipped with armored vehicles, the attack was rejected and the retreat continued towards Rapallo. On the 26th the column passed the Ruta Pass, where it was again attacked by the Americans who lost a Scherman hit by the anti-tank of the "Cadelo". Once in Recco he headed towards Uscio, where on the 27th the order was given to destroy weapons, material, vehicles, cannons, stocks, keeping only the individual armament, continuing the march along mountain paths. The direction of travel is towards the Scoffera, after passing it you can try to reach the Po Valley and the Po. In the afternoon of April 27, 1945, completely surrounded by American forces, the "Aosta" Group, together with the other departments of the "Pasquali He surrendered to the Americans and received the honor of arms.

First Commander of the Group, Major Collaridi, then Major Colonna, then Captain Mondini, finally Captain Bruno Folli.

### 2nd Artillery Group "Bergamo"

The "Bergamo" artillery group, armed with 12 Skoda 75/13 howitzers of the I G.M. already in service

in the Royal Army Groups, it was established in Pavia on 1 January 1944, incorporated into the 1st Alpine Artillery Regiment, and transferred to Germany to train in the Feldstetten camp. He returned to Italy at the end of July and took up a position in Liguria in support of the 1st Alpine Regiment, placing himself south of Uscio. During their stay in the area, the batteries of the "Bergamo" did not sustain any major fighting, only patrol activities in search of partisans and airplanes by the Allies and the participation, with patrols and sections of howitzers, in some round-up operations towards Torriglia and Bobbio. A piece was detached at the Passo del Bocco and remained there, reinforcing the garrison formed by a platoon of Alpini, until the end of the hostilities. Once the danger of landing on the Ligurian coast returned, following the landing in Provence in France, in October the "Bergamo" Group began preparations to move to the Garfagnana front. It came online, staggered, between 27 and 29 October, and was immediately engaged in supporting the 1st Company of "Aosta" involved in the attack of the F.E.B. Once the defensive line was restored, the "Bergamo" assumed the definitive deployment in support of the left sector, with the 4th Battery in Palleroso, the 5th in Fosciandora, the 6th in San Carlo first, then at the Fosciandora bridge and finally at the Piani di Riana , the Battery Command was positioned in Bucchia. Of great importance for the activity of the batteries of the "Bergamo", were the advanced observatories, placed in the front line, and also in the no man's land, which will allow, for the entire stay of the Group in Garfagnana, to identify and strike with the utmost precision and less waste of ammunition the enemy targets. To remember the famous "Banana 41", observatory located on the slopes of Mount Perpoli, that of Treppignana, that between Pian del Rio and Colle. The howitzers of the "Bergamo", with precise fire actions, took part in all the actions to counter the offensives launched by the Americans of the 92nd "Buffalo" Division from mid-November to the end of December, actively participated in the "Wintergewitter" offensive at the end of 1944 and remained in line until the beginning of April 1945 demonstrating, in five months of line, the great ability of the Alpine gunners, who developed precise, targeted and timely fire actions, such as to receive the congratulations of the German Commands. From February the "Bergamo" acted in support of the Bersaglieri of the "Italy" Division, which came on line to replace the "Monterosa", "San Marco" and Germans. In early April, the "Bergamo" received the order to move to the front of the Western Alps in Piedmont, thus rejoining the rest of the Division deployed there. While moving towards La Spezia, along the Campori - Casola di Lunigiana - Pallerone route, on 11 April he received the order to return quickly to Garfagnana to help the "Italy" Division which risked being surrounded by the Americans who had broken through the front. in Massa. It then became the flying artillery of a Combat Group, formed by the 1st Company of the Bersaglieri Battalion "Mameli", by the Battalion of the 2 Bersaglieri Regiment "Italy" Division and by the "Bergamo" itself, called "Ferrario" from the name of the Commander of the 1st Battalion, which fought in Soliera, then in Fivizzano, then headed towards the Cerreto Pass and then returned back and headed towards the Cisa. Then began the path towards the end: Fivizzano, Soliera, Pallerone, Aulla, Pontremoli, always compact and always under bombardment, by the planes and the American artillery which, with the medium calibers, had reached a short distance and fired along the Street. On 24 April in Pontremoli the Group escaped yet another aerial bombardment that killed the columns folding in the road, then, after having sabotaged the pieces and the carts, the folding continued towards the Cisa Pass. On the evening of the 27th General Carloni ordered the "Intra" and "Bergamo" to set up a Combat Group with the task of forcing the passage over the Taro bridge. The next morning the action was successful but shortly after, near Medesano, the first Brazilian avant-gardes showed up. The "Bergamo" then withdrew to Fellegara, where the equipment and mules with a small escort were left, and then continued on to Medesano. On 28 April, in the morning, the "Bergamo" Group put an end to its war activity and surrendered to the Brazilians in Fornovo Taro.
Commander of the Group, the Captain (later Major) Giuseppe Anzil.

## 3rd Artillery Group "Vicenza"

The Vicenza Artillery Group, armed with 12 Skoda 75/13 howitzers of the I G.M. already in service in the Groups of the Royal Army, it was established in Pavia on January 1, 1944, as the "Verona" Artillery Group (subsequently changing its name to that of "Vicenza" on August 17, 1944), and incorporated into the 1st Alpine Artillery Regiment . Transferred to Germany, he trained in the Heuberg and Gaensewag camps, from where he returned to Italy and arrived there on 20 July. It was deployed in Liguria, in the Riviera di Levante, as an anti-landing function, in the Leivi area above Chiavari in support of the 1st Regiment. On the 26th one of his trucks was attacked by the partisans but, after this episode, he had no more opportunities for clashes with the rebels, not even participating in the round-up operations at the end of August. The batteries had the pieces pointed towards the coast and awaited the landing of the enemy. Once the anti-landing requirement ceased, since the "Bergamo" was also present in support of the 1st Regiment, the "Vicenza" was transferred to Piedmont, in the Province of Cuneo, in the Stura Valley, where it replaced German units. The Command was placed in Argentera and the Batteries, in defense of the Colle della Maddalena, were positioned in French territory: the 7th in Val Lanzargner, the 8th in Val del Rio du Pis, the 9th in Val Puriac, from where it had to move to Ferriere because the opposing batteries of Barcelonette had discovered and taken under fire. With the onset of snow, the passes became impassable and the Batteries were moved back towards the valley, in Italian territory, in the winter locations. The Command was placed in Sambuco, near Pietraporzio, the 7th and 8th Batteries came on this side of the Colle della Maddalena taking up position in the valley, the 9th went to San Bernolfo. There was no particular war activity, not even the partisans created excessive nuisance, only during the winter did the activity of inciting desertion increase and it was necessary to recall the baggage station located in Demonte to the Group Headquarters. During the winter, about twenty partisans and draft evaders came to the Group to be drafted. At the beginning of April 1945 the "Vicenza" was ordered to move to Val Varaita and Val Maira, in support of the "Bassano" Battalion. The preparations had already begun and the quartermaster's quarters were already in place but the precipitate of events blocked the transfer. On 24 April the "Vicenza" went down to San Dalmazzo in Cuneo where the Command of the "Littorio" Division left each department free to decide on its own conduct. The "Vicenza" destroyed the guns, abandoned the mules and, with only light armament, headed on lorries to Turin, in a column with departments of the "Littorio" and other formations. Passing through Racconigi and Venaria Reale, the column, weakly opposed by the partisan forces, reached the free zone of Strambino Romano, continuing to Ivrea where it disbanded on 2 May 1945.

First Commander of the Group, Captain (later Major) Pietro Gheza, then Captain (later Major) Alessandro Foli, then Captain Roberto Santini.

## 4th Artillery Group "Mantova"

The "Mantova" Hippotrained Artillery Group, armed with 12 Fh18 105 German howitzers [6], was established in Pavia on 1 January 1944, incorporated into the 1st Alpine Artillery Regiment, and transferred to Germany to train in the Heuberg and Munsingen camps. He returned to Italy at the end of July, siding in Liguria, as an anti-landing function, in the Coreglia area, in the left division of the "Monterosa" in support of the 2nd Regiment. With its howitzers, the "Mantova" was destined to support the pieces of the "Aosta" Group, positioned along the coast, in contrast to the forces eventually landed on the Ligurian beaches. During his stay in Liguria, no particularly significant events occurred in the confrontation with the partisans, apart from the usual ambushes and ambushes that were not particularly violent. At the end of October, the "Mantova" was transferred to the Garfagnana front, where it arrived in line in the first days of November and was deployed north of Castelnuovo, straddling the Serchio river, in the sector from Fosciandora to Pontardeto, with the

---

6 Carlo Cornia, in his book "Monterosa. Storia della Divisione Alpina Monterosa della R.S.I.", mentions the initial presence of 12 100/17 howitzers in charge of the "Mantova" Group. From further publications, photographic evidence and testimonies of veterans, the presence of the German howitzers FH18 - 10.5 is certain.

Command deployed in Pieve Fosciana, the 10th Battery located in Pontardeto, the 11th to the west of the Pieve, the 12th to the north of Castelnuovo in the river bed. He participated in all the defensive and offensive fighting in the sector, during the "Wintergewitter" offensive at the end of 1944, his firing actions were particularly appreciated by the Germans, so much so that he received written praise from the German Command. In February 1945 he left the Garfagnana front to be transferred to Piedmont, on the front of the Western Alps. The transfer of the "Mantova" was rather laborious, due to the weight of the howitzers and support equipment. From Garfagnana the Group reached Liguria and then Turin, from where it headed towards Val Susa in early February. It remained in the area for a few weeks, then, on March 30, the Command, the 10th and the 11th Battery headed towards Montgenèvre, where they took up positions. The 12th was instead sent, on March 29, to the Aosta Valley, taking sides in La Thuile to defend the Piccolo San Bernardo, under the tactical dependence of the 4th Alpine Regiment of the "Littorio" Division responsible for the defense of the sector. The "Mantova" had been in line for just over a month when, following the collapse of the front of the Gothic line, it received the order to withdraw towards the plain. On April 26, the Command, the 10th and 11th Batteries joined the column formed by the "Tirano", and by German units of the 5 "Gams", descending the Val Chisone towards Pinerolo, from where they continued, only with the Alpini of the "Tirano", Towards Orbassano, where the gunners accepted the surrender agreed with the CLN local. As soon as he laid down his arms, the shootings of the prisoners began immediately. Almost all of the fallen in the "Mantua", which should be remembered had not carried out any counter-guerrilla activity, was caused by the shootings. The 12th Battery, deployed in the Aosta Valley, on April 26, with the fire of its howitzers, effectively countered a further French attempt to descend into the valley, thus remaining in line until May 7. On May 8, 1945 he surrendered to the Americans. Commander of the Group, Major Salvatore Pace.

## "Cadelo" Divisional Exploration Group

The Exploring Group was formed in Vercelli, in January 1944, with Bersaglieri from the 4th Regiment of Turin and the 5th Regiment of Siena as the XXIII "Crimson Flames" Exploring Group. In the same month he was placed in the 4th "Monterosa" Alpine Division, as an explorer department, then transferred to Germany where he trained in the Feldstetten camp. Returning to Italy at the end of July, he was deployed to Borzonasca with the functions of divisional reserve. At the end of August, he participated in the great operation for the safety of the communication routes behind the anti-landing deployment. Starting from Borzonasca he marched towards Rezzoaglio and reached Santo Stefano d'Aveto on the 28th, after some battles against the partisan forces and overcoming significant road interruptions, capturing a significant amount of weapons and vehicles. After this operation it remained a garrison in the Aveto Valley with headquarters in Rezzoaglio and garrisons in Santo Stefano. At the end of September he detached a garrison platoon at Passo del Bocco. On 27 September, in Santo Stefano d'Aveto, with the classic partisan ambush, Major Cadelo, Commander of the Group, was killed. In his honor from that day the Exploring Group took its name: "Gruppo Exploring Cadelo". In early November, following the passage of a large part of the "Vestone" to the partisans, he carried out roundups in the Barbagelata area, recovering Alpini, weapons, ammunition and quadrupeds. At the end of October it was transferred to the Garfagnana front where, from November 2, when it reached Piazza al Serchio it was assigned to the divisional reserve function. But just two days later, on November 4th, he sent in line first a platoon of the 2nd squadron, then the whole squadron and then moved there in full. It was deployed to the west of the Serchio river in the sector: Sassi - Eglio - Monte Grottorotondo - Le Rocchette, joining the Alpini of the "Intra" and the marines of the II Battalion "Birds" of the "San Marco" Division, on the Case Pozza - Case line Cornola, with the cannon platoon, with four 75/27 cavalry pieces, placed in Eglio. Unfortunately, the defensive line was very thin, since the positions, defended by 4 or 5 Bersaglieri, were two or three hundred meters away from each other. He actively participated in the defensive fighting following

the American offensives in November, for the reconquest of the 832, 1029, 1031 and 1068 quotas reached by the Americans, then counterattacked the enemy deployment with deep patrols. At the end of November, the 2$^{nd}$ Squadron suffered some attacks by the partisans which led to the capture of many Bersaglieri and the loss of some positions. The technique adopted was always the same: partisans disguised as Bersaglieri or Alpini approached the positions and as soon as they entered them they took the military prisoners. Following the recovery of a correspondence of a partisan brigade, it came into possession of the names of four officers of the "Cadelo" who were in contact with the partisans: three were captured and one managed to escape. From that moment the attacks against the men of the "Cadelo" ended. In December he actively participated in the failure of the offensive, launched on the 12$^{th}$ by the Americans of the 92$^{nd}$ "Buffalo" with the support of the partisans operating behind the defenders, aiming to conquer an altitude of 832. During the "Wintergewitter" offensive at Christmas 1944, The "Cadelo" was destined to make one of the four demonstration bids provided for in the attack plan. Calomini was occupied almost immediately, bypassed Vergemoli and, crossing the Turrite di Gallicano, reached Fornovolasco and Trassilico, thus continuing with the activity of patrols deep within the enemy lines, in the area of Trombacco. During these operations, a company of Bersaglieri from the 1$^{st}$ "Italy" Division was added to the "Cadelo", the first unit of this Division to reach the front. From the end of the Christmas offensive until February 1945, the "Cadelo" remained deployed in the positions prepared on the new defensive line. At the beginning of February he was replaced in line by the III Battalion 1$^{st}$ Bersaglieri Regiment "Italia" Division, starting the transfer to Liguria. During the journey he was sent to support the 148$^{th}$ Division, to reoccupy some positions in the Massa sector, and finally arrived on 23 February in Liguria, placing the Command and two Squadrons between Terrarossa and Borgonuovo and the other Squadron in Sestri Levante. In mid-March he carried out a roundup inland towards the Apennine Passes. On 24 April the "Cadelo" met in Chiavari with the other Departments of the "Monterosa", under the command of Colonel Pasquali, and began to withdraw towards the Po, in columns with them. On April 25$^{th}$, 26$^{th}$ and 27$^{th}$ he fought rearguard fights against the American avant-gardes on the Entella and on the Ruta. On April 27 north of Uscio he surrendered with the honor of arms.
First Commander of the Group, Major Girolamo Cadelo, then Captain Gustav Weintz, then Lieutenant Colonel Emanuele Andolfato, finally Major Villa.

## Divisional Units

### Training Battalion
This Battalion was set up with the aim of training the personnel who arrived in Munsingen, in October 1943, which would subsequently be used for the education of recruits according to the German training model. It carried out its activity from mid-November until the early months of 1945, when the staff was assigned directly to the departments within the Division. First Commander of the Battalion, Lieutenant Colonel Zanocco, later Lieutenant Colonel Giuseppe Alberton.

### "Ivrea" Battalion
It was established in Aosta on 1 February 1944 and assigned to the "Monterosa" Division as Complements Battalion. After completing his training in the Munsingen camp, he returned to Italy at the end of July, to be deployed in Liguria in Borgonovo Ligure, behind the coastal array, with functions as a divisional reserve. His 2$^{nd}$ Company was included in the "Saluzzo" Battalion and shared its fate until the dissolution of the Battalion at the end of September, thus returning to the "Ivrea" staff. He always remained in the area, carrying out security tasks in the rear areas, communication routes and garrison and anti-partisan struggle, until April 24, 1945, when he received the order to prepare the retreat towards the Po, where, according to the plans prepared, he would had to assume the defense of the Casteggio sector. The fate followed on April 25 from Chiavari with the other

departments of the Division. The marching column, after fighting on the Entella and on the Passo della Ruta, moved towards the Passo della Scoffera but was intercepted by the troops of the 442$^{nd}$ Nippo-American Regiment. On April 27, 1945 the "Ivrea" surrendered with the honor of arms.
First Commander of the Battalion, Major Raffaello Faccioli, later Captain Giambattista Bonemazzi.

## Pioneers Battalion

It was established in Asti on 1 February 1944 and assigned to the "Monterosa" Division. Transferred to Germany, he completed his training partly in Germany and partly in Austria. Back in Italy, he deployed a Company in Carasco as a divisional reserve, while the other two were located one for each of the defensive sectors, with the task of providing for the construction of fortifications. In November the Command, the 1$^{st}$ Company and a Platoon of the 2$^{nd}$ were sent to the Garfagnana front, while the rest of the 2$^{nd}$ Company remained in Liguria until the end of hostilities. The 3$^{rd}$ Company was employed in Santo Stefano Lodigiano for the construction of fortifications and ferry operations on the Po, then it was transferred to Piedmont, to Ivrea, where it disbanded in April 1945. Upon returning from the Garfagnana front, the 1$^{st}$ Company was sent to Valle d'Aosta where he presided over the Runaz Gallery until the end of April 1945.
First Commander of the Battalion, the Captain (later major) Virio Agamemnon, later Major Taggiasco.

## Connections Battalion

It was established in Pavia on 1 January 1944 and assigned to the "Monterosa" Division. After completing his training in Germany, in the Esslingen camp, he returned to Italy setting up the radio centers and telephone networks in the Ligurian sector pertaining to the Division. It was then deployed on the front of the Garfagnana and on the front of the Western Alps, in Piedmont, in the area of Ivrea.
Battalion commander, Captain Antonio Janesch.

## Transportation Battalion

It was established in Milan on 1 February 1944 and, after being assigned to the "Monterosa" Division, transferred to Germany to be trained at the Munsingen, Esslingen and Boblingen camps. Returning to Italy, he was deployed in the Cicagna area with detachments in the divisional subsectors of the coastline. Transferred to the Garfagnana front at the end of October, he set up his base in Bagnone, in Lunigiana, and detachments in Piazza al Serchio and Torrite di Castelnuovo. At the beginning of 1945 he was sent to Piedmont, moving to Castellamonte.
First Commander of the Battalion, Major Guidoboni, then Captain Giuliano Cossutta, then Captain Giustetta, finally Captain Zoppi.

## Divisional Antitank Company

Established in Verona on January 26, 1944, it completed training in the Feldstetten camp returning to Italy at the end of July, where it was deployed as a divisional reserve in the surroundings of Chiavari. At the end of October she was transferred to the Garfagnana front, where she competed with her men to defend the resistance line and the Christmas offensive. In February 1945 she was transferred to Piedmont. First Commander of the Company, Captain Borra, subsequently Lieutenant Raffaele Lucci.

## Health Department

It was formed by the Healthcare Company set up in Alessandria on December 5, 1943 and by the Hospital Units, the Surgical Unit and the Ambulance Section set up in Milan on February 1, 1944. After training, he returned to Italy, siding in Liguria with the 1$^{st}$ Company in Cicagna and the 101$^{st}$ Company first in Castiglione Chiavarese then in Piacenza. In October 1944, the whole Department was transferred to the Garfagnana front, between Camporgiano and Bercelo, where the backward divisional hospital was located. After the Garfagnana, the Health Department was transferred to Piedmont on the front of the Western Alps, relocating with the 1st Company in Castellamonte and the 101st Company in Aosta, with a small detachment at the Piccolo San Bernardo. Commanders of the Health Department, Captain Dr. Mario Micheletti of the 101st and Captain Mario Mucci of the 1st.

## Intendency
Established in Alessandria on 5 December 1943, and assigned to the "Monterosa" Division, after training in Munsingen it returned to Italy, in Liguria, relocating the various companies along the Val Fontanabuona. Following the new deployment assumed by the Division, on the Garfagnana front it set up a divisional logistic center in Bagnone, while, in Piedmont, it was located in the Castellamonte area. The Veterinary Company, established in Alessandria on 1 February 1944, was initially deployed in Uscio in Liguria, then in Monticelli Terme and finally in Brescia, where it concluded the retreat at the end of April 1945 and broke up.

## "Vestone" Battalion
The "Vestone" Battalion was formed in August 1944, with a staff comprising: a Command Department, four light companies (each equipped with three heavy machine guns and three light guns) and the support of a Mortar Platoon sold by "Brescia", grouping the four alarm companies set up by drawing personnel from the organic Battalion of the 2nd Alpine Regiment, with the aim of maintaining control of the communication and supply roads from the coastline to the resistance line along the Apennine ridge, through the Passi di Scoffera, Bocco, Madonna delle Nevi, Hundred Crosses. He participated in the great roundup operation at the end of August and operated as a mobile unit in the rear of the Division. On the night between 3 and 4 November, in Torriglia, in the Genoese hinterland, the Commander of the Battalion, in agreement with some officers, handed over three of the four Companies to the partisans. 120 men, belonging to the fourth Company, deployed outside Torriglia, escaped capture, as well as some Alpini who managed to escape from the partisans, while about 200 were captured. Among these only about fifty, with the Commander and some officers, remained with the partisans, the others preferred to return home, while others returned to the Division. Commander of the Battalion, Major Paroldo.

## "Saluzzo" Battalion
The "Saluzzo" Battalion was constituted, towards the middle of August 1944, by bringing together the two alarm companies of the 1st Alpine Regiment, formed with elements from the organic Battalion, to the 2nd Company of the "Ivrea" with the aim of maintaining control of the communication and supply roads in the rear of the Division. He took part in the great round-up operation at the end of August and was stationed in Bobbio, establishing the garrison there with the Command, with a Company detached in Marsaglia and a Platoon at the Penice Pass. During the offensive unleashed by the partisans in September, who attacked the isolated garrisons and Varzi, the Company deployed in Marsaglia, thanks to the Commander, was handed over to the partisans (about fifty Alpini did not return to the Division), the Platoon detached at the Passo del Penice was overwhelmed after running out of ammunition, by Bobbio the "Saluzzo" did not intervene, in support of the 2nd Company of the "Brescia" surrounded by Varzi, citing the lack of forces as an excuse. In the face of these events, the Division Command ordered an investigation and on 28 September the "Saluzzo" Battalion was dissolved. The 2nd Company of the "Ivrea" returned to the original Battalion, while the surviving Alpini returned to their Battalion of belonging of the 1st Regiment.
Commander of the Battalion, Major Dalla Valle.

▲ On 16 July 1944 the Duce Benito Mussolini inspects the wards of the "Monterosa" Division fully deployed in the Munsingen field (Monterosa Historical Photographic Archive).

▼ Alpini of Monterosa receive the visit of Marshal Rodolfo Graziani in Nervi Monterosa Historical Photographic Archive).

▲ After reviewing the "Monterosa", Mussolini delivered a heartfelt speech and handed the battle flags to the Regiments. Alongside Mussolini, General Carloni, commander of the Division (Archivio Storico Photo Associazione Monterosa).

▶ Colonel Giorgio Milazzo, who was first commander of the 2$^{nd}$ Alpine Regiment and, later, last commander of the entire "Monterosa" Division (Monterosa Historical Photographic Archive).

▼ Alpini of the Connections Battalion. The department was established in Pavia in January 1944 and, after being assigned to the "Monterosa Division, was trained in Germany at the Esslingen field (Monterosa Historical Photographic Archive).

▲ A Platoon of Pioneers from the "Aosta" Battalion engaged in the refurbishment of a bridge in Val Maira (Monterosa Historical Photographic Archive).

▲ Alpini of the 9th Company of the "Bassano" Battalion of the 1st Alpine Regiment in Casteldelfino.

▼ Alpini attend the 1944 Christmas Mass under the San Veran Pass (Monterosa Historical Photographic Archive).

▲ Two officers of the "Monterosa" Division photographed in the winter of 1944: interesting the use of a camouflage jacket, made with Italian M1929 fabric by the soldier on the right (Crippa).

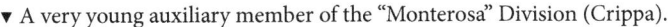

▲ Pair of three-pointed green flames used on the collar of the jacket by the Alpini of the "Monterosa".
▼ A very young auxiliary member of the "Monterosa" Division (Crippa).

▲ Group photo for some Bersaglieri of the "Cadelo" Exploring Group (Monterosa Historical Photographic Archive).

▼ Alpine troops of the Baracca Presidium in Liguria (Monterosa Historical Photographic Archive).

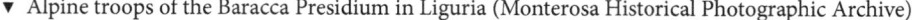

▲ The 2nd Platoon of the 7th Company of the "Morbegno" Battalion, together with soldiers of the 102nd Compagnia Cacciatori Carro, at the Baracca garrison (Monterosa Historical Photographic Archive).

▼ Soldiers of the 2nd Platoon of the 7th Company of the "Morbegno" Battalion posing next to a minefield (Monterosa Historical Photographic Archive).

▲ Alpine troops of the "Monterosa" Division engaged in the construction of fortifications in Liguria (Monterosa Historical Photographic Archive).

▲ Unusual but captivating shot for this machine gunner of the "Monterosa" Division (Crippa).

# MONTEROSA

## COMBATTERE!

▲ The first page of issue 7 of the newspaper "Monterosa", published by the same Division.

▲ Mortar post of the Alpini of the "Monterosa" on the first line of the front in Garfagnana.
▼ In what would appear to be a simple chicken coop, there is actually piece number 3 of the 6$^{th}$ Battery of the 2$^{nd}$ "Bergamo" Someggiato Artillery Group, cleverly disguised to appear as a building (Monterosa Historical Photographic Archive).

▲ Two Alpini busy arranging and cleaning their uniforms in a position in Garfagnana (Monterosa Historical Photographic Archive).

# Soldati della "MONTE ROSA" e della "SAN MARCO"

I tedeschi hanno ordinato di mettervi in linea affinchè truppe tedesche siano libere di essere gettate contro gli Alleati nel settore orientale del fronte italiano.

Anche per un'altra ragione le truppe tedesche sono state ritirate: la posizione da loro abbandonata ed ora occupata da voi sarà con ogni probabilità isolata fra poco.

Quale sarà allora il vostro destino? La scelta è a voi: morte, disfatta, deportazione in Germania, o resa immediata.

Ora vi trovate a combattere contro i vostri connazionali. State lottando dalla parte che perde, dalla parte che irrevocabilmente dovrà subire la disfatta. Che sarà di voialtri se un giorno la disfatta sarà diventata realtà? Con l'avanzata degli Alleati si faranno anche i conti con i traditori dell'Italia.

— **Voi state combattendo dalla parte che perde! Passate dalla parte che vince!**

▲ The Allies often resorted to psychological warfare against their enemies. One of the most used weapons was the throwing of leaflets written in the language of the opponents, which were intended to induce fear and discourage the soldiers, such as this leaflet used in Garfagnana (Monterosa Historical Photographic Archive).

▲ An artillery column from the "Monterosa" Division advances into the Stura Valley (Monterosa Historical Photographic Archive).

▼ One of the 75/13 howitzers in service at the "Monterosa" Division ready to fire (Monterosa Historical Photographic Archive).

▲ Alpine Artillerymen of the III Someggiato Artillery Group "Vicenza" in a moment of rest (Archivio Storico Photo Associazione Monterosa).

▼ The transport of the cannons of the "Monterosa" Division was carried out mainly according to the best traditions of the Alpine troops. The pieces were in fact donned or horse-trailed by the faithful companions of the Alpine artillerymen, the mules (Monterosa Historical Photographic Archive).

▲ The command of the 2nd Platoon of the 14th Company of the "Tirano" Battalion in Cresta Rascià (Monterosa Historical Photographic Archive).

▼ Officers of the "Tirano" Battalion of the "Monterosa" Division in the famous ski resort of Sestriere (Monterosa Historical Photographic Archive).

▲ Group of Alpini of the "Tirano" Battalion, photographed in the harsh winter 1944 - 1945 (Monterosa Historical Photographic Archive).

▼ The war is over: the Alpini of the "Monterosa" Division are taken prisoner by the Brazilian soldiers of the F.E.B. and are sent to the allied prison camps (Manes).

▲ After the Second World War, Don Adamo Accorsa, former chaplain at the "Monterosa" Division, built a church in Celle di Varzi, a small hill town in the province of Pavia, with the ruins left by the fury of the war, to promote peaceful coexistence between men, of any nation and any political creed. In the early 1950s he began his work, helped and encouraged by the apostolic Nuncio Monsignor Angelo Roncalli, the future Pope John XXIII. Inside the touching religious monument, called the "Temple of the Fraternity of Peoples", there are also four metal plaques, placed in memory of the 4 Divisions of the Republican National Army (Crippa).

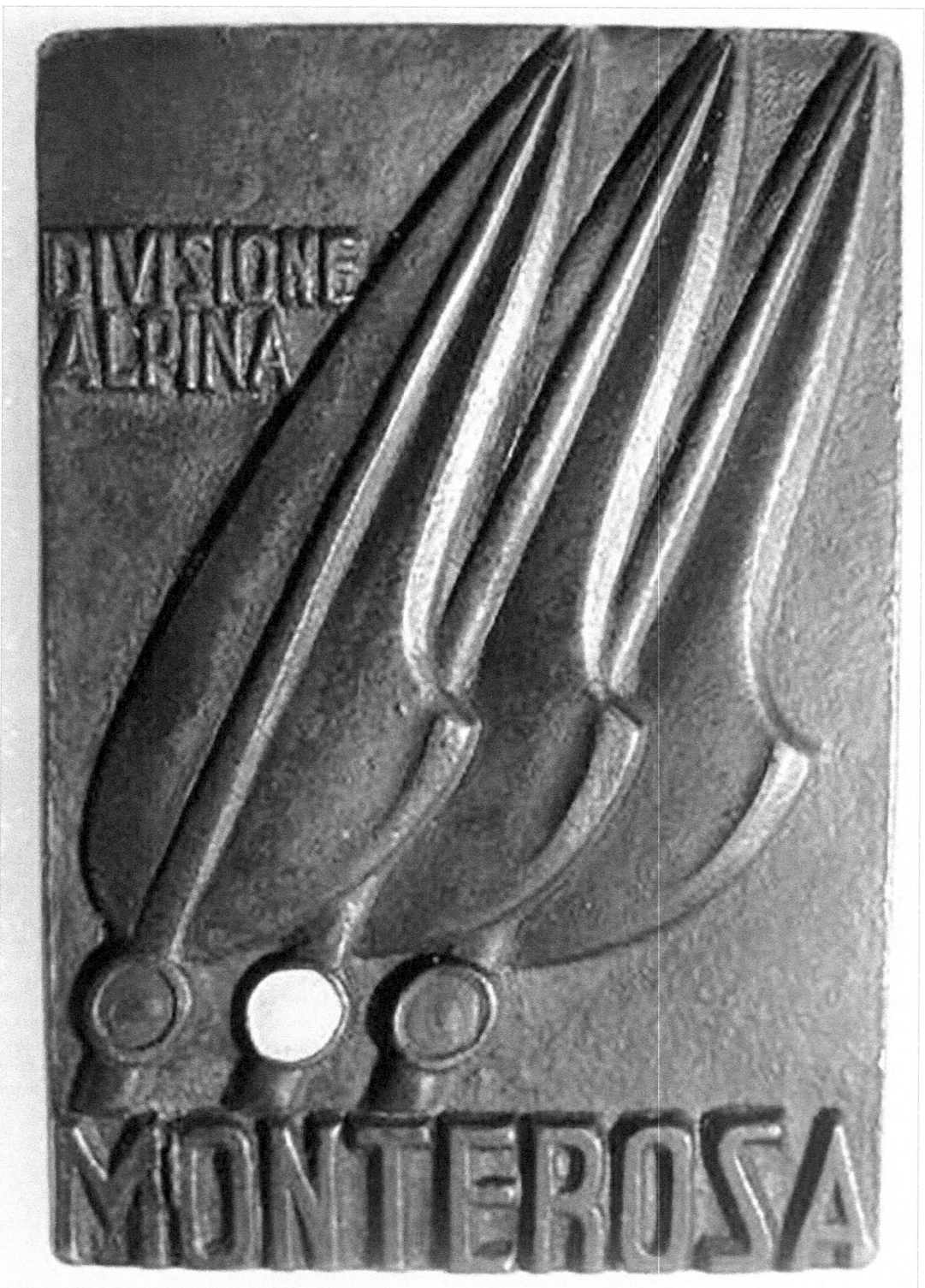

▲ The pin for the "Monterosa" Division was coined by the Lorioli company in Milan: this is the first version, in the next version the wording was changed to "1st ALPINE DIVISION MONTEROSA". When the numbering of the Division was changed 4 th the brooch was never changed (Monterosa Historical Photographic Archive).

# Bibliography

## Books

- AA.VV., "Repubblica Sociale Italiana - Storia", Centro Editoriale Nazionale, Roma, 1959.
- AA.VV., "Soldati e Battaglie della Seconda Guerra Mondiale", Hobby & Work Italiana Editrice, Bresso (MI), 1999.
- Arena Nino, "L'Italia in Guerra 1040/45", Ermanno Albertelli Editore, Parma, 1997.
- Arena Nino, "R.S.I. – Forze Armate della Repubblica Sociale – La guerra in Italia – 1943 – 1944 – 1945", Ermanno Albertelli Editore, Parma, 2002.
- Associazione Divisione Monterosa, "I nostri Caduti, noti e ignoti", tipografia Campi, Milano, 1999.
- Baldrati Pieramedeo, "La San Marco sulla Linea Gotica", Soldiershop, Zanica (BG), 2020.
- Baldrati Pieramedeo, "San Marco... San Marco – Storia di una Divisione", Associazione Divisione Fanteria di Marina San Marco, Milano, 1989.
- Cornia Carlo, "Monterosa – Storia della Divisione Alpina 1944 - 1945", Ermanno Albertelli Editore, Parma, 1998.
- Costantini Maurizio, "La seconda battaglia delle Alpi – Agosto 1944 Maggio 1945", Roberto Chiaramonte Editore, Collegno (TO), 2000.
- Crippa Paolo, Cucut Carlo, "Reparti Alpini nella RSI", Soldiershop, Zanica (BG), 2019.
- Crippa Paolo, Cucut Carlo, "Reparti Bersaglieri nella RSI", Soldiershop, Zanica (BG), 2019.
- Cucut Carlo, "Le Forze Armate della R.S.I. 1943 – 1945 – Forze di terra", G.M.T., Trento, 2005.
- Cucut Carlo, "Forze armate della R.S.I. sul confine occidentale", Marvia Edizioni, Voghera (PV), 2009.
- Cucut Carlo, "Forze armate della R.S.I. sulla linea Gotica", Marvia Edizioni, Voghera (PV), 2011.
- Cucut Carlo, Bobbio Roberto, "Attilio Viziano – Ricordi di un corrispondente di guerra", Marvia Edizioni, Voghera (PV), 2008.
- Del Giudice Davide, "La linea gotica tra la Garfagnana e Massa Carrara 1944/1945", Ritter Edizioni, Milano, 2003.
- Del Giudice Davide, "Il Battaglione Intra sulle Alpi Apuane", Edizioni Centro Grafica Stampa, 1997.
- Fabbri Marcello, "Il sergente che non poteva morire. Con il battaglione «Ivrea», divisione Monterosa. Storie e fatti 1944-45", Lo Scarabeo, Milano, 2004.
- Fiaschi Cesare, "La guerra sulla linea gotica occidentale. Divisione Monterosa 1944-45", Editrice Lo Scarabeo, Bologna, 1999.
- Kuchler Hein, "Fregi mostrine distintivi della RSI", Intergest, Milano, 1974.
- Lamura Riccardo, "Il gruppo esplorante della Divisione "San Marco" nelle langhe durante la R.S.I.", Ritter Edizioni, Milano, 2009.
- Lombardi Andrea, "La Controbanda: Storia e esplorazioni del III Gruppo Esploranti arditi e della Controbanda di Calice Ligure, divisione F.M. San Marco", Soldiershop, Zanica (BG), 2017.
- Pisanò Giorgio, "Gli ultimi in grigioverde", Edizioni F.P.E., Milano, 1967.
- Pisanò Giorgio, "Storia della Guerra Civile in Italia", Edizioni F.P.E., Milano, 1965.
- Rocco Giuseppe, "Con l'Onore per l'Onore – L'organizzazione militare della R.S.I. sul finire della Seconda Guerra Mondiale", Greco & Greco Editori s.r.l., Milano, 1998.
- Sandri Leonardo, "Il Corpo d'Armata "Lombardia" – Armeekorps "Lombardia" – Agosto 1944 – Maggio 1945", Edito in proprio, Milano 2019.

- Scarone Emilio, "Battaglione Alpini Cadore nella R.S.I.", Novantico Editore, Pinerolo (TO), 2000.
- Sparacino Fausto, "Distintivi e medaglie della R.S.I. 19343/45 della Legione SS Italiana dei veterani della R.S.I.", EMI, Milano, 1994.
- Sparacino Fausto, "Distintivi e medaglie della R.S.I. 19343/45", EMI, Milano, 1988.
- Zucconi Ernesto, "Divisione Monterosa", Novantico Editore, Pinerolo (TO), 1996.

## Magazines and publications

- Conti Arturo, "Albo caduti e dispersi della Repubblica Sociale Italiana", Fondazione della
- R.S.I. – Isti-tuto Storico, Terranuova Bracciolini (AR), 2018.
- Scalpelli Adolfo, "La formazione delle forze armate di Salò attraverso i documenti dello
- Stato Maggiore della R.S.I." in "Il movimento di liberazione in Italia" issues 72 e 73, I.N.S.M.L.I., 1963.
- "Acta", various issues, Fondazione della R.S.I. - Istituto Storico, Terranuova Bracciolini (AR).
- "Uniformi ed armi", various issues, Ermanno Albertelli Editore, Parma.
- Ministero Forze Armate, "Istruzione provvisoria sull'uniforme dell'Esercito Nazionale Repubblicano", Tipografia FF. AA., Anno XXII (1944).
- "Monterosa", magazine of Associazione Reduci Divisione Alpina "Monterosa", various issues.
- "San Marco", magazine of Associazione Reduci Divisione "San Marco", various issues.

# TITLES ALREADY PUBLISHING

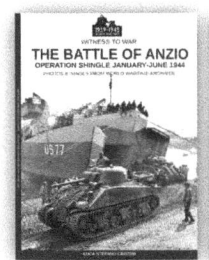 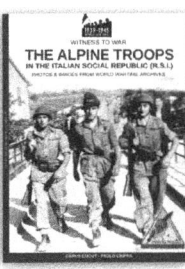 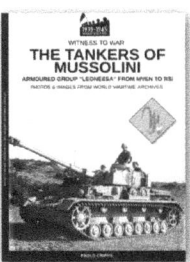  

BOOKS TO COLLECT

www.ingramcontent.com/pod-product-compliance
Ingram Content Group UK Ltd.
Pitfield, Milton Keynes, MK11 3LW, UK
UKHW050411240426
12048UKWH00020B/1463